Country Cooking

with Evelyn

Evelyn Timmermann

NORTEX PRESS  Austin, Texas

Evelyn's Hobbies Unlimited
San Antonio, Texas

Front cover, left to right: Evelyn's Best Pecan Pie, p. 84; Evelyn's Best White Bread, p. 7; Delicious Banana Pie 1945, p. 86; Apple Caramel Cake, p. 28; Grandma's Cream Puffs, p. 58; Golden Butter Cake (doubled recipe), p. 26, filled with Evelyn's Cream Filling, p. 30, and iced with Coconut Pecan Filling & Icing (Delicious), p. 30; Evelyn's Texas Carrot Cake, p. 15; Peach Crisp Dessert, p. 68; and Evelyn's Peach Upside Down Cake, p. 16.

FIRST EDITION
Copyright © 2003
By Evelyn Timmermann
Manufactured in the U.S.A.
By Nortex Press
A Division of Sunbelt Media, Inc.
Austin, Texas
ALL RIGHTS RESERVED.

ISBN 0-9709124-1-2

I created this cookbook hoping all will enjoy it from cover to cover. I wrote this book because of all the enjoyable hours I have spent in the kitchen preparing meals. I love to plant a garden. I enjoy canning, freezing and dehydrating vegetables and fruit that my garden produces, plus I purchase some when they are in season.

I was born and grew up on a farm and have lived on the farm most of my life. I know what a hearty appetite a hard working-person can acquire, so good food is always appreciated.

I have had some people tell me: "I can't cook. I try but nothing tastes good." This book is for the experienced and the beginner. When you are hoping to make a good impression on family or friends, I know all of my recipes will bring you joy and good eating. Within these pages you will find new and old recipes and a lot of hand me downs.

Although I know some of you will make changes for your family's tastebuds, in this book you will find the general idea. I have done a lot of experimenting with recipes, had some failures, had some very successful and tasty recipes. My husband, being the kind of good guy he is, has always been honest with his tastebuds. So I have printed my best recipes.

I have prepared this cookbook as a tribute to all who love to cook and those who want to cook because a good cook keeps the world going with good healthy food. Everybody needs good food.

This cookbook has taken me years to collect recipes and lots of hard work to write, but I have enjoyed every minute of it. I hope this cookbook will bring you lots of compliments and enjoyment as it has brought me.

Plus, I want to say thanks to my husband and all my friends who encouraged me to publish this cookbook.

Thank you,
Evelyn Timmermann

Contents

Breads, Rolls, Biscuits & Polska Goodies

Evelyn's White or Jalapeño Bread

2 cups scalded milk (110° to 115°)   3 tablespoons shortening
4 tablespoons sugar   2 tablespoons salt
3 packets yeast

Mix all the above ingredients together in an electric mixer. Mix in 11½ cups flour total but you need to divide the flour. Put in enough flour in the above to make a thick mixture, when the electric mixer can't knead anymore.

1. Knead in the rest of the flour by hand.
2. Place dough in greased bowl and cover until double in bulk about 1½ hours.
3. Punch down fold over edges and let rise about 30 minutes.
4. Divide in four balls and cover; let rise about 15 minutes. Shape into loaves.
5. Place in 4 greased loaf pans; let rise 1 hour and 15 minutes.
6. Bake in preheated oven 375° for about 35 minutes.

For jalapeño bread:

1 cup onion (chopped fine)   1 lb. Cheddar cheese (shredded)
1 lb. jalapeño peppers (cut up)

Soak jalapeño peppers in hot salt brine (¾ cup hot water and ¼ cup salt) while preparing the onion and cheese. When ready for the peppers, drain and rinse the salt off the peppers. Mix the 3 above ingredients in the bread dough when kneading. Continue steps.

Use: 7½ cups of 1 brand of flour and 4 cups of another brand, canning salt to soak the peppers, purple onions for color, red and green jalapeño for color. Can also add 1 small jar pimientos drained well, for color.

Evelyn's Bread Coins (Texas Style)

Mix a recipe of Evelyn's Best White Bread. Let rise till double in size. Then divide into 6 balls. Knead a different seasoning in each ball.

Example: garlic and herb, jalapeño, Creole and Cajun seasoning and Nature's Seasons. Whatever you want.

Roll each ball into a long strip, about as thick as a nickel. Place each strip on a greased cookie sheet, far enough apart so they don't touch when they bake. Bake at 350° till done.

When cool, with electric knife slice about ⅛-inch thick, scatter on cookie sheet, and return to oven to toast the best little snack in Texas.

Evelyn's Bread Crumbs
Made in bread machine

Measure with bread machine cup

1 cup wheat flour	1 cup rye flour

1 cup potato and corn and white flour mixed (3 different flours)

3 tablespoons sugar	1½ teaspoons salt
1 pkg. yeast	1½ tablespoons vegetable oil
5 oz. water	5 oz. milk
1 tablespoon dry milk	3 tablespoons onion flakes
Sprinkle of jalapeño	1½ teaspoons dry tomatoes
1½ teaspoons dry celery	1½ teaspoons dry garlic

Bake as a loaf of bread, then slice and cube and put in oven to toast. Put in blender to make bread crumbs. May be used to dip or coat different meats, seafood, etc.

Apple Breakfast Discover

½ cup water (110°)	2½ teaspoons yeast
1 cup milk	½ cup sugar
1 egg	3 tablespoons vegetable oil
3½ cups flour	2 teaspoons vanilla
½ teaspoon salt	

Beat with mixer and dough hooks. Put in greased bowl. Let rise 1½ to 2 hours. Divide dough in half; place each half in greased 9-inch pie plate.

Mix 1 can apple pie filling with ¼ cup corn starch. Divide in half; spread half on each dough, sprinkle sugar and cinnamon on top. Let rise again, about 45 minutes. Bake at 375° about 30 minutes.

Drop Buttermilk Biscuits

Preheat oven to 425°

2 cups flour	2 teaspoons sugar
¼ teaspoon salt	½ cup butter
1 tablespoon baking powder	1¼ cups buttermilk
½ teaspoon cream of tartar	

Mix all dry ingredients, cut in butter, and add buttermilk. Stir until just blended. Divide dough into 7 pieces. Drop dough into greased biscuit pan. Bake 15 to 19 minutes. Makes 7 biscuits.

Old Fashion Corn Bread

1½ cups cornmeal
2½ teaspoons baking powder
3 tablespoons sugar
2 eggs
1 teaspoon bread gluten

4 tablespoons flour
½ teaspoon salt
3 tablespoons vegetable oil
1 cup milk

Bake at 350° in a greased 9-inch pan for 20 to 25 minutes.

Royalty Corn Bread

2 eggs
1 cup milk
1 teaspoon salt
½ cup sour cream

1½ teaspoons baking powder
1 cup self-rising flour
1½ cups corn meal
3 tablespoons melted butter

Beat all liquid ingredients. Mix all dry ingredients. Beat all together very well. Then add:

1 cup shredded Cheddar cheese
½ cup chopped onion

¼ cup red bell pepper
1½ teaspoons dry jalapeño

Stir all ingredients together very well. Pour into a foil-lined 13 x 9 x 2-inch pan sprayed with non-stick spray. Bake at 375° for 40 minutes or till brown.

Jalapeño Corn Bread

1½ cups cornmeal
2½ teaspoons baking powder
3 tablespoons sugar
2 eggs
1 teaspoon bread gluten
½ cup diced onion
1 cup shredded Cheddar cheese

4 tablespoons flour
½ teaspoon salt
3 tablespoons vegetable oil
1 cup milk
1 teaspoon Cajun and Creole spice
¾ cup chopped jalapeño peppers

Mix all ingredients very well. Bake at 350° in a greased 9-inch pan for 20 to 25 minutes.

Optional: *If you like the flavor and color, but don't want all the fire of a jalapeño, put the ¾ cup of jalapeños in ¾ cup of boiling water and ¼ cup of salt, and let them soak till you are ready to add them to your recipe, then drain and rinse.*

Country Dinner Rolls

¾ cup water
3 cups bread flour
6 tablespoons sugar
3 tablespoons dry milk

1 egg beaten
1½ teaspoons salt
6 tablespoons butter
2 teaspoons yeast

Put in bread maker set on dough, remove and let rest 20 minutes. Make little balls about the size of a quarter. Put 3 into each muffin tin pan compartment. Let rise till double. Bake at 350° for 10 to 15 minutes.

Speckled Corn Bread

1½ cups popcorn cornmeal (got to grind popcorn yourself)
4 tablespoons flour
½ teaspoon salt
1 egg
1 cup milk

2 teaspoons baking powder
3 tablespoons vegetable oil
3 tablespoons sugar

Mix all together. Pour into greased 9-inch pan. Bake at 350° for 20 or 25 minutes or till golden brown.

1950 Golden Corn Bread

1 cup yellow corn meal
¼ cup sugar
4 teaspoons baking powder
1 cup milk

1 cup flour
½ teaspoon salt
¼ cup soft shortening
1 egg

Mix and beat all together; bake in greased muffin tins or 8-inch square pan. Bake at 350° for 20 to 25 minutes.

1940 Jalapeño Corn Bread

1 cup yellow corn meal
1 teaspoon baking powder
1 teaspoon sugar
1 cup canned cream style corn
¼ lb. shredded Cheddar cheese
½ cup vegetable oil

½ cup flour
1 teaspoon salt
2 eggs
1 med. onion chopped
½ cup jalapeño peppers
1 cup buttermilk

Preheat oven to 350°. Grease an 8-inch pan. Sift together all dry ingredients. Beat the eggs, oil and milk; add the dry ingredients. Stir in the cheese, onions, corn and peppers. Bake 25 to 30 minutes.

Evelyn's Best White Bread
Made in bread machine

1¾ teaspoons yeast
1½ teaspoons salt
¼ cup dry milk
¼ cup shortening or butter (solid)

1½ tablespoons bread gluten
¼ cup sugar
3 cups bread flour
1¼ cups water

Optional: Instead of water use ¾ cup sour cream and ½ cup milk

Bake in bread machine on bread setting.

Optional: Instead of baking your bread in the bread machine, set your machine on dough. Then take dough out, shape into a loaf, and put in greased bread pan. Let rise, and bake at 375° for 30 to 35 minutes.

White Delicious Bread
Made in bread machine

Medium loaf
  1¼
  2
  1
  1
  1
  1
  ¾ cup + 2 tablespoons
  1

Large loaf
1½ teaspoons yeast
3 cups bread flour
1½ teaspoons salt
1½ tablespoons sugar
1½ tablespoons dry milk
1½ tablespoons solid shortening
1¼ cups water
1½ tablespoons gluten

Bake in bread machine.

Note: Time and temp. to bake loaf of bread: 375° for 30 to 35 minutes.

Best Whole Wheat Bread
Made in bread machine

1 cup water
¼ cup butter or solid shortening
1½ teaspoons salt
1½ teaspoons bread machine yeast
2 cups bread flour

1 egg beaten
2 tablespoons sugar
¼ cup dry milk
1 tablespoon bread gluten
1 cup whole wheat flour

Bake in bread machine. Delicious—rises so high.

Old Time Country Corn Bread

1½ cups cornmeal
1½ teaspoons baking powder
1 teaspoon soda
2 eggs
1 cup milk

4 tablespoons flour
½ teaspoon salt
3 tablespoons vegetable oil
3 tablespoons sugar

Pour dough into a greased 9-inch cake pan. Bake at 350° for 20 to 25 minutes.

Evelyn's Popcorn Cornbread

2 eggs
½ cup sour cream
1½ teaspoons baking powder

1 cup milk
1 cup self-rising flour
1 teaspoon salt

1½ cups popcorn corn meal (you will have to grind your own)
3 tablespoons melted butter

Beat all liquid ingredients. Mix all dry ingredients; mix all together very well. Bake at 350° for 30 minutes or till done.

Old Farmer Biscuits

2 cups flour (sifted)
3 tablespoons shortening
⅔ cup water or milk

4 teaspoons baking powder
1½ teaspoons salt

Blend flour, shortening, baking powder and salt. Add liquids; mix well. Roll out and cut with biscuit cutter, and place on greased baking sheet. Bake at 425° till golden brown.

For Cheese Biscuits

Use the above recipe. Add ¾ cup Cheddar cheese and ¼ cup chopped onion.

Polska Goodies Ten Day Starter
Starter for Corn Bread, Coffee Cake and Pecan Bread

To start the starter from scratch, do the following:

1 cup milk
1 cup sugar
1 cup flour
¾ teaspoon yeast

Mix with wooden spoon only (no metal) in glass or plastic bowl only (no metal). From Day 1 to Day 5 the starter may be stored in a Ziploc bag, squeeze the bag and release the air every day.

On Day 6 when you add the 1 cup sugar, 1 cup flour, 1 cup milk. Store the starter in a ½ gallon bottle. With an ice pick punch about 8 holes in the lid to release fermentation. Then set the bottle into a bowl, in case of a runover. Every day remove the lid and stir down with wooden spoon. Never refrigerate.

Day 10 add 1 cup of each flour, sugar and milk. Bake or start Day 1. Makes 4 cups. You need 1 cup per batch. All 3 pages are giving these same directions. when you no longer need the starter for a while put in Ziploc bag, 1 cup per bag, and freeze it, till you need it again.

When you remove it from the freezer, bake with it or start Day 1 and add nothing. On Day 6 add 1 cup flour, 1 cup sugar and 1 cup milk. Use starter for coffee cake, corn bread and pecan bread.

Day 1: do nothing.
Day 2: squeeze the bag and release the air.
Day 3: squeeze the bag and release the air.
Day 4: squeeze the bag and release the air.
Day 5: squeeze the bag and release the air.
Day 6: add 1 cup flour, 1 cup sugar, and 1 cup milk.
Day 7: rotate the bottle and release the air.
Day 8: rotate the bottle and release the air.
Day 9: rotate the bottle and release the air.
Day 10: combine in a large bowl, the batter and add 1 cup flour, 1 cup sugar, and 1 cup milk. Mix with wooden spoon or spatula. To start starter again, take 1 cup starter and start Day 1.

The above makes 4 cups: Make 3 starters; take 3 Ziploc bags and pour 1 cup starter in each bag; save you one for next time and give the other two to your friends, with the instructions. If you don't give your starter away, you may use it any day, from Day 1 to Day 5. But be sure to keep one at all times for the starter.

To the remaining 1 cup of starter in the bowl, bake the following: Coffee Cake, Cornbread or Pecan Bread.

Ten Day Polska Coffee Cake

1 stick butter
3 eggs
2 cups flour
1 tablespoon white corn syrup

1¼ cups sugar
½ cup milk
3 teaspoons baking powder
1 cup starter from page 9

Add extracts:
½ teaspoon butternut
¼ teaspoon maple
½ teaspoon almond
1 teaspoon rum

½ teaspoon caramel
½ teaspoon vanilla nut
½ teaspoon butter pecan
1½ teaspoons vanilla

Mix topping well:
¼ cup sugar
1½ cups pecans (chopped)

1 teaspoon cinnamon

With mixer, cream butter and sugar. Add milk, eggs, extracts and starter. Sift flour, baking powder; add to creamed mixture. Pour half the batter into a greased 13 x 9 x 2¼-inch pan and sprinkle half the topping over the batter. Add the remaining batter, and sprinkle the remaining topping on the batter. Bake at 350° for 1 hour. Test with wooden pick for doneness.

Complete directions for making polska coffee cake.
1. Beat till smooth: eggs, milk, white corn syrup and extracts.
2. Mix together: flour, sugar and baking powder.
3. Add: butter and flour mixture, to step 1. Beat till smooth.
4. Add: starter to the batter and beat smooth.
5. For topping, mix: sugar, cinnamon and pecans.
6. Line a 13 x 9-inch pan with foil and spray with nonstick spray. Pour ½ the batter and sprinkle ½ the topping on top.

Pour the other half of batter on top and sprinkle the rest of the topping. Bake at 350° for 55 to 60 minutes.

Ten Day Polska Corn Bread

1½ cups cornmeal
1 teaspoon salt
3 eggs
3 tablespoons oil
¾ cup Cheddar cheese
2 tablespoons sugar

¾ cup flour
3 teaspoons baking powder
½ cup milk
½ cup onion
1 teaspoon dry jalapeño peppers
1 cup starter from page 9

Sift the cornmeal, flour, salt and baking powder. Beat the eggs. Cream the starter, milk and oil. Add the eggs and sifted ingredients and beat. Stir in the onions, cheese and jalapeño. Pour into greased 13 x 9-inch pan. Bake at 350° for 50 minutes. About the last 15 minutes cover with foil to prevent over browning.

Ten Day Polska Pecan Bread

1 cup oil
2 cups flour
1 cup sugar
1 teaspoon vanilla
3 large eggs
½ teaspoon salt
1 cup starter from page 9

½ cup milk
1 teaspoon vinegar
2 sm. boxes instant vanilla pudding
2½ teaspoons baking powder
1 teaspoon cinnamon
1 cup chopped pecans

Mix all dry ingredients together. Beat the eggs, milk, oil, vanilla and vinegar together. Then beat all together. Pour into 2 large loaf pans, well greased, sprinkled with flour.

For topping: Mix ¼ cup sugar and 1 teaspoon cinnamon. Sprinkle cinnamon and sugar on top if desired. Bake at 325° for 1 hour.

Keep this as a daily guide for starter:

Day 1: do nothing
Day 2: squeeze the bag
Day 3: squeeze the bag
Day 4: squeeze the bag
Day 5: squeeze the bag
Day 6: add 1 cup flour-sugar-milk
Day 7: rotate the bottle
Day 8: rotate the bottle
Day 9: rotate the bottle
Day 10: 1 cup flour-sugar-milk-bake

Cakes, Brownies, Cheesecakes & Frostings

Evelyn's Texas Carrot Cake

Preheat oven to 350°

2⅛ cups flour
3 teaspoons baking powder
1 teaspoon cinnamon
5 eggs
1 cup sugar
1 cup brown sugar
1 ¼ cups butter
1 teaspoon almond

1 teaspoon butter pecan
1 apple (peeled and chopped fine)
2 cups carrots (shredded)
1 8-oz. can crushed pineapple (drained)
¾ cup coconut
1 cup pecans (chopped)
1 tablespoon vanilla

Mix flour, baking powder and cinnamon. Beat eggs and sugars till fluffy. Add butter and flavorings; beat till smooth. Add flour mixture and beat. Beat in carrots, pineapple, coconut and apple; stir in pecans.

Prepare 2 (9-inch) cake pans with nonstick spray. Divide the dough evenly in the 2 pans and spread and bake for 40 minutes. Or 9 x 13-inch pan with nonstick spray, bake for 60 minutes.

Frosting:
8 oz. cream cheese
4¼ cups powdered sugar
1 teaspoon danish pastry extract

1 stick margarine
2 tablespoons condensed milk
2 teaspoons vanilla

Beat all together till very smooth about 3 minutes. Spread on cake; decorate with pecans.

Chocolate Malt Cake

2 cups heavy cream
4 eggs
⅓ cup sugar
1½ teaspoons vanilla

¼ teaspoon salt
¼ cup baking cocoa
2½ teaspoons baking powder
1⅔ cups all purpose flour

Beat the eggs, sugar, cream and vanilla. Mix the flour, baking powder, salt and cocoa together. Add to the egg mixture. Pour into a greased 9 x 12-inch cake pan. Bake at 350° for about 35 minutes or till wooden pick comes clean.

Apple Pie Cake

¼ cup butter
¾ cup sugar
1 cup flour
½ teaspoon cinnamon
¼ teaspoon salt
2½ cups apples (sliced)

4 tablespoons condensed milk
2 large eggs
1 teaspoon baking powder
½ teaspoon nutmeg
2 teaspoons vanilla
Whipping cream

Cream butter and sugar; beat well. Add eggs, combine all liquid and dry ingredients and beat well; add sliced apples. Pour into a greased 9-inch pie plate. Bake at 350° for 35 to 45 minutes. Top with whipped cream.

Evelyn's Peach Upside Down Cake

Foil line a 9 x 13-inch cake pan; spray with nonstick spray. Put in bottom of pan:

¾ cup brown sugar
1 cup chopped pecans

3 to 4 cups fresh peaches

Mix together the following:
1 yellow or white cake mix
1 stick butter
5 whole eggs for yellow cake or 5 egg whites for white cake
1 heaping teaspoon baking powder
1 teaspoon vanilla nut extract
1 cup water
1 teaspoon butter extract
1 envelope dry whipped topping
1 teaspoon vanilla

Pour the above over the peaches and bake at 350° for 1 hour or till inserted wooden pick comes clean. Remove from pan when cool. Spread top of cake with your favorite pie filling (1 can), strawberry or apple or cherry, and whipped topping.

Delicious Flan Cake

1 yellow cake mix

Mix according to directions on box. Divide batter into 2 greased flan pans. Bake at 350° for 35 minutes.

Flan filling:
1 can apple filling (cut apples smaller)

Flan topping:
1 16-oz. frozen whipped topping
1 sm. box vanilla instant pudding

Beat till stiff, spread on top of apple filling. Bring the frozen whipped topping up slightly on edge and arrange fresh strawberries in center.

Yummy Flan Cake

This is enough to fill 2 flan pans.

1 yellow cake mix	¼ cup coconut dessert mix
½ teaspoon butter pecan extract	¼ cup grapeseed oil
1 teaspoon baking powder	1¼ cups water
4 large eggs	

Pour into 2 greased flan pans. Bake at 350° for 35 minutes.

Flan filling: *This is enough for 1 flan only.*

½ cup coconut dessert mix	½ cup sugar
1½ cups milk	½ teaspoon vanilla

Cook till thick, stirring constantly. When cool, pour on flan.

Flan topping: *This is enough for 1 flan only.*

16 oz. frozen whipped topping	1 sm. box vanilla instant pudding
½ teaspoon butter pecan extract	

Beat till stiff. Put in cake decorator and decorate top of flan.

Hint: *Bake cake in a shiny pan. Bake at 350° for best results.*

Evelyn's Master Cake Mix

8 cups cake flour	1 cup dry milk
3 tablespoons plus 1 teaspoon sugar	2 teaspoons salt
3 tablespoons plus 1 teaspoon baking powder	

Additionals for 1 cake:

3 cups Evelyn's Master Cake Mix	1½ cups sugar
1 envelope dry whipped topping	4 large eggs
2 teaspoons vanilla	1 stick butter

Pour into 13 x 9 x 2-inch cake pan or two 8- or 9-inch cake pans sprayed with nonstick spray. Bake in convection oven at 325° for about 25 minutes or till inserted wooden pick comes clean. Or bake in regular oven at 350° for about 35 minutes or till inserted wooden pick comes clean.

Southern Jelly Roll Cake

1 cup sifted cake flour
¼ teaspoon salt
¼ cup cold water

3 teaspoons baking powder
3 eggs
1 cup sugar

Beat the above ingredients. Pour into wax paper lined 10 x 15-inch pan. Bake at 425° for 12 to 15 minutes. Turn cake onto wax paper and roll while hot. When cool, unwrap and spread your favorite jelly and roll again.

For a chocolate jelly roll cake use:
¾ cup cake flour   ¼ cup baking cocoa

Lazy Cake

Layer the following in oblong baking dish:

2 cups crushed pineapple and juice
1 sm. box reg. vanilla pudding
¾ cup coconut
½ box white cake mix (1 layer)

½ cup sugar
1 cup pecans
1 cup miniature marshmallows
½ cup water poured on top

Bake at 350° for about 30 minutes.

Evelyn's No Citrus Fruitcake

3½ cups flour
1 cup sugar
1 teaspoon baking powder
½ cup shortening
1 cup strawberry preserves
1 teaspoon rum extract
½ cup cherry syrup from cherries
¾ cup cherries (cut in half)

1½ cups brown sugar
5 large eggs
1 can condensed milk
2½ sticks butter
1 tablespoon vanilla
1 cup (8 oz.) chopped dates
1 cup dried cranberries
1 cup dried apples (cut up)

2 ½ cups (14 oz.) dried mixed fruit (cut up), remove the prunes
4 cups pecans

Mix together the flour, sugars and baking powder. Mix all the dried fruit, cherries and pecans together. Beat the eggs, preserves, cherry juice, extracts, butter, shortening and milk. Add the flour mixture to the egg mixture, and beat. Fold in the fruit and pecan mixture.

Pour into a greased 9 x 12-inch air pan. Bake at 300° for 15 minutes then at 325° for 2 hours and 15 minutes. Last 1 hour and 30 minutes cover with foil. Bake till wooden pick inserted comes clean.

Evelyn's Piña Colada Cake

1 white cake mix
1 cup of 15-oz. can cream of coconut
¼ cup vegetable oil
4 large eggs

1 3¾-oz. box vanilla cook pudding
1 teaspoon rum extract
1 pkg. dry whipped topping
1 teaspoon baking powder

Beat the above. Stir in: 4 oz. can crushed pineapple, drained.

Pour into a greased 9 x 13-inch pan. Bake at 350° for about 35 minutes or until wooden pick inserted in center comes clean.

Topping:
4 oz. crushed pineapple, drained
rest of the cream of coconut

1 can condensed milk

While cake is warm poke holes in cake with a wooden spoon handle, and pour over cake evenly; cool.

Icing:
12 oz. frozen whipped topping
4 oz. crushed pineapple, drained

½ cup coconut

Beat the whipped topping, coconut and pineapple. Frost cake.

The Farmers Cake

1 cup flour
1 stick margarine
1 cup pecans
1 cup powdered sugar
8 oz. cream cheese

1 cup coconut
2 sm. pkgs. instant coconut pudding
3 cups milk
3 cups frozen whipped topping
2 teaspoons vanilla

First: Mix flour, margarine and pecans together till crumbly; press into a 9 x 13-inch greased pan. Bake at 350° for 20 minutes. Cool.

Second: Cream sugar and cream cheese. Fold in 1 cup frozen whipped topping and spread over first layer. Sprinkle with coconut.

Third: Layer mix pudding and milk spread over second layer.

Fourth: Top with frozen whipped topping, garnish with coconut and pecans.

Like Family Delicious Cake

Yellow cake mix (mixed according to directions)

1 small box instant vanilla pudding
1 cup chopped pecans
½ cup brown sugar
1 teaspoon baking powder

1 cup shredded apple
1 teaspoon cinnamon
2 teaspoons vanilla

Put in bundt pan and bake according to cake mix instructions. Or put in 9 x 13-inch pan and bake according to cake mix directions.

1990 Everyday Fudge Cake

1 cup flour
2 tablespoons baking cocoa
¼ teaspoon salt
2 tablespoons vegetable oil
1 cup pecans (stir in batter)

¾ cup sugar
2 teaspoons baking powder
½ cup milk
1 teaspoon vanilla

Mix the above till smooth. Pour batter into a 9 x 9 x 2-inch greased pan. Mix the 2 following ingredients:

1 cup brown sugar

¼ cup baking cocoa

Spread the brown sugar/baking cocoa on top of the batter.

1 ¾ cups hot water

Pour the hot water over the batter. Bake at 350° for 40 minutes. Let stand 15 minutes.

World's Best Pineapple Cake

1 cake mix yellow or white with pudding (bake according to directions)

Topping:
1 can condensed milk
1 (20 oz.) can crushed pineapple (put in strainer and press to drain)
1 (8 oz.) frozen whipped topping

When cool, punch holes in cake with wooden spoon handle. Spread the condensed milk over cake, then spread the drained pineapple over cake. Spread frozen whipped topping over cake and refrigerate.

Chocolate Dream Cupcakes

1 box chocolate or white cake mix (18.5 oz.)
1 cup water   ⅓ cup buttermilk
2 teaspoons vanilla   2 eggs

Filling:
8 oz. cream cheese   ½ cup sugar
1 large egg   ½ teaspoon salt
3 tablespoons baking cocoa   ½ cup pecans

Preheat oven to 350°. In large bowl, combine cake mix, water, buttermilk and vanilla mix until well blended. Add 2 eggs one at a time, beating after each addition, until well blended and smooth. Spoon mixture into greased or paper-lined muffin tins, filling each cup half full.

In medium bowl, beat together cream cheese and sugar until light and fluffy. Beat in 1 egg, salt and cocoa. Drop 1 tablespoon cheese mixture on each cupcake. Sprinkle with pecans. Bake for 25 or 30 minutes.

Lillian's Apple Fruit Cake

2½ cups flour   2 cups sugar
2 teaspoons vanilla   1 teaspoon allspice
3 apples shredded   3 large eggs
2 cups pecans   1 cup butter
2 tablespoons baking cocoa   1 teaspoon cinnamon
½ cup water   1 teaspoon soda

Mix soda and water together. Then combine all ingredients. Bake at 350° for 60 minutes or till wooden pick inserted comes clean.

Evelyn's Italian Cream Cake

1 stick butter   ½ cup shortening
2 cups sugar   5 large eggs (separated)
2 cups self-rising flour   2 teaspoons baking powder
1 cup buttermilk   2 teaspoons vanilla
½ cup coconut   1 cup pecans

Cream butter and shortening, add sugar and beat till smooth. Add egg yolks and beat well; combine flour and baking powder. Add mixture alternately with buttermilk. Stir in vanilla, coconut and pecans. Fold in beaten egg whites. Pour in 3 greased 9-inch cake pans. Bake at 350° for 25 minutes. Top with Evelyn's Italian Cream Frosting on page 33.

Net-Gla-Eve Pear Cake

3 large eggs   2 cups sugar

Cream together the above.

2 cups flour   2 teaspoons vanilla
1½ teaspoons baking powder   1 teaspoon cinnamon
½ teaspoon apple bake spice   ½ teaspoon salt
1 cup vegetable oil

Combine the above and beat 2 minutes. Stir in:

3 cups fresh pears sliced very thin   ½ cup pecans chopped

Put in a greased bundt pan or square pan or oblong pan. Bake at 350° for 1 hour 15 minutes. *Optional:* In food processor slice fresh or frozen pears with the thick slice blade; drain in colander, cover with wax paper till needed.

Fruit Roll or Jelly Roll Cake

1 box angel food cake mix (mix according to directions)

Line jelly roll pan with waxed paper, spray with nonstick spray. Spread batter in pan. Bake at 375° for 10 to 12 minutes. When cake is done loosen from pan and sprinkle powdered sugar on cake and roll up. Let cool 20 minutes.

2 cups whipping cream   3 tablespoons powdered sugar
1 quart strawberries sliced

Beat the whipping cream and powdered sugar until soft peaks form. Put half the cream in the cake and half of the strawberries and roll up. Put the other half of the cream and strawberries on top and sides of the cake.

1977 Margie's Pumpkin Cake

3½ cups sifted flour   2 teaspoons soda
1½ teaspoons salt   1 teaspoon cinnamon
1 teaspoon nutmeg   3 cups sugar
⅔ cup water   1 cup oil
2 cups pumpkin (1 can)   ½ cup pecans

Beat all ingredients into a smooth batter. Pour into a greased long cake pan, or three 1 lb. coffee cans. Bake at 350° for about 50 minutes.

Pecan Pie Cake

1 box plain white cake mix   ½ cup melted butter
4 large eggs

Remove ⅔ cup of batter from above. Set aside.

½ cup brown sugar (packed)   2 teaspoons vanilla
2½ cups chopped pecans   1½ cups light corn syrup

Preheat oven to 325°. Beat together the cake mix, butter and 1 egg. Spread the remaining batter in a greased 13 x 9 x 2-inch glass pan. Bake for 25 minutes or till lightly brown. Cool for 15 minutes. Leave oven on.

Beat the reserved ⅔ cup batter, corn syrup, sugar, 3 eggs and vanilla. Fold in pecans. Pour the mixture over the warm cake in the pan. Bake for 40 or 45 minutes until edges are browned but middle is still soft; cool.

1977 Margie's Banana Pudding Bundt Cake

2 bananas   1 box yellow cake mix
1 sm. box vanilla instant pudding   4 eggs
1 cup water   ¼ cup oil
½ cup pecans

Beat bananas; add remaining ingredients. Pour into a greased and floured 10-cup bundt pan. Bake at 350° for 60 to 70 minutes.

Pineapple & Carrot Cake 1977

3 cups flour   2 cups sugar
1 teaspoon cinnamon   1½ teaspoons soda
½ teaspoon salt   2 teaspoons baking powder
2 cups grated carrots   1½ cups vegetable oil
3 eggs   2 teaspoons vanilla
1½ cups pecans
1 8-oz can crushed pineapple (drain and save juice)

Mix all dry ingredients together. Beat eggs and pineapple juice. Add dry ingredients. Stir in pineapple, carrots and pecans. Pour into a greased bundt pan. Bake at 325° for 1½ hours.

Good Tomato Soup Cake

½ cup shortening
2 eggs
2 teaspoons baking powder
½ teaspoon cinnamon
1 can = 1 cup tomato soup

1½ cups sugar
2 cups flour
¼ teaspoon soda
½ teaspoon nutmeg
½ cup nuts

Mix all together, pour into two 9-inch greased pans. Bake at 375° for about 30 minutes.

Topping:
1 (3-oz.) cream cheese
2 teaspoons milk

½ teaspoon vanilla
2½ cups powdered sugar

Mix all together and spread on cool cake.

Special -L- Chocolate Cake

2 cups flour
½ cup baking cocoa
⅔ cup shortening
1 cup buttermilk
½ teaspoon salt
3 eggs

1¼ cups sugar
½ cup water
1 teaspoon baking powder
2 teaspoons soda
½ teaspoon cinnamon
1 teaspoon vanilla

Cream shortening, sugar and eggs. Add soda to milk alternately; add dry ingredients. Beat all till smooth. Makes 3 (9-inch) layers. Bake at 350° for 30 minutes.

1950 Feather Jelly Roll Cake

3 large eggs
5 tablespoons water
1 teaspoon baking powder

1 cup sugar
1 cup sifted cake flour
¼ teaspoon salt

Preheat oven to 375°. Mix all ingredients together. Pour onto wax paper-lined 15 ½ x 10 ½ x 1-inch pan. Bake 12 to 15 minutes.

When done, loosen edges and turn upside down on towel sprinkled with powdered sugar and roll up. When cool, unroll and spread with favorite jelly or filling and reroll.

1949 Aunt Annie's Potato Cake

2 cups sugar
1 cup butter
4 large eggs
1 cup mashed potatoes
3 teaspoons cocoa
½ cup milk
1 teaspoon cinnamon

1 teaspoon nutmeg
1 teaspoon cloves
1 cup chopped pecans
2 cups cake flour
2 teaspoons baking powder
1 teaspoon vanilla

Bake at 350° for 1 hour.

1945 Febronia's Raw Apple Cake

Cream together:
2 cups sugar   1 cup solid shortening
4 large eggs (beat in 1 at a time in above mixture)

Add:
½ cup water with 1 teaspoon soda dissolved
1 ½ teaspoons vanilla

Sift and add to above:
2 cups flour with 2 tablespoons cocoa

Stir in:
1 large apple chopped   1 cup chopped dates
1 cup pecans

Bake at 350° till wooden pick inserted in center comes clean.

Rave Rewards Cake

1 yellow cake mix
1½ cups water
½ stick margarine or butter
1 cup pecans

1 sm. box vanilla instant pudding
4 large eggs
1 cup coconut
1 teaspoon baking powder

Pour into 3 greased 9-inch cake pans. Bake at 350° for about 35 minutes.

Supreme Coconut Cake

1 box yellow cake mix (18-¼ oz.)

Bake two 9-inch layers according to cake mix directions.

Filling:

2 cups sour cream   2 cups sugar
1½ cups coconut

Mix the sour cream and sugar very well. Stir in the coconut; filling will be soft. Set aside 1 cup of the filling for the frosting. Cut each layer in half. Put ⅓ of the filling between the layers.

Icing:

8 oz. frozen whipped topping   1 cup reserved filling

Fold the whipped topping and filling together to frost cake.

Evelyn's Peach Cake

1 large can peaches drained or fresh peaches
1 cup pecans

Grease 13 x 9 x 2-inch pan and layer it with the peaches and pecans.

2 cups biscuit and pancake mix   ¾ cup sugar
2 eggs   ¾ cup milk
2 tablespoons vegetable oil   2 teaspoons vanilla

Beat the 6 above ingredients. Pour over the peaches and pecans. Bake at 350° for 40 minutes.

Golden Butter Cake

⅓ cup butter   ¾ cup sugar
1 large egg   1 teaspoon vanilla
½ teaspoon almond   1⅓ cups flour
1½ teaspoons baking powder   ½ teaspoon salt
⅔ cup milk

Combine butter, sugar, egg and flavoring. Beat on high speed 5 minutes. Mix all dry ingredients together, add alternately with milk, beating on low speed of mixer. Pour into a greased 8 x 8 x 2-inch pan. Bake at 325° for 20 to 25 minutes.

Evelyn's Layered Cake

Layer the following in oblong baking dish:

2 cups crushed pineapple and juice
2 small boxes reg. vanilla pudding
1 cup coconut
1 cup miniature marshmallows
1 14-oz. can condensed milk, spread on top
1 cup water, poured on top

1 cup sugar
2 cups pecans
1 box white cake mix

Bake at 350° for 30 minutes. Mix the batter with a fork till all ingredients are moist. Bake another 40 minutes.

Granny's Pear Walnut Spice Cake

4 large eggs
2 cups flour
2 teaspoons vanilla
2 teaspoons baking powder
½ teaspoon ground cloves
2 cups chopped pears
1 cup walnuts

1½ cups sugar
1 cup butter
1 teaspoon salt
1 teaspoon cinnamon
½ teaspoon allspice
1 cup pecans

Bake at 350° for 45 to 60 minutes.

Holiday Eggnog Cake

3 tablespoons butter
1 18½-oz. yellow cake mix with pudding
1 cup eggnog
1 teaspoon rum flavoring

2 large eggs

¾ teaspoon nutmeg
1 teaspoon baking powder

Preheat oven to 325°. Spray bundt pan with nonstick spray. Mix all ingredients. Beat about 3 minutes. Pour into pan. Bake about 1 hour, or till wooden pick inserted comes clean.

Glaze:
½ stick butter
1 teaspoon rum flavoring

½ cup sugar

Put in saucepan on medium heat and stir till sugar melts; pour over cake.

Gelatin Cake

Prepare white cake mix, per package directions. Bake cake in a 13 x 9 x 2-inch pan as directed. Cool for 30 minutes. Poke holes in cake with wooden spoon handle, about 1 inch apart. Pour the following mixture over cake:

¾ cup boiling water   1 small box of your favorite gelatin
½ cup cold water

Topping:
1 envelope whipped topping mix   1 box instant vanilla pudding mix
1 ½ cups cold milk   2 teaspoons vanilla

Whip for 7 minutes. Refrigerate till cake is cool. Then spread on cake.

Apple Caramel Cake

1 ¾ cups brown sugar packed   2 cups flour
1 teaspoon cinnamon   ½ teaspoon salt
2 teaspoons baking powder   1½ sticks butter
1 tablespoon vanilla   3 eggs
2½ cups apples (shredded)   1½ cups pecans (chopped)

Preheat oven to 350°. Spray 10- or 12 -inch bundt pan with nonstick spray and sprinkle with flour. Beat all ingredients together (except pecans). Beat about 2 minutes on high speed of mixer, stir in pecans. Pour into bundt pan. Bake for about 1 hour or until wooden pick inserted comes clean. Cool.

Glaze with:
½ stick butter   ½ cup brown sugar
2 teaspoons vanilla

Put the 3 ingredients in a saucepan over medium heat. Stir till sugar is melted. Pour over cake.

Farm Heaven Icing

¼ cup condensed milk   1 pkg. dry whipped topping
¼ cup margarine   ½ cup whipping cream
½ teaspoon coconut flavoring   4 cups powdered sugar
½ teaspoon almond flavoring

Beat till fluffy.

Coconut Cream Cheese Frosting 50's

4 tablespoons butter
1 3-oz. cream cheese
4 cups powdered sugar

2 cups coconut
¼ cup evaporated milk
2 tablespoons butter

Melt butter in skillet; add coconut, stir constantly until golden brown. Cool, and add rest of ingredients. Spread on cake.

Brown Butter Icing

¼ cup butter
3 tablespoons cream
½ cup pecan halves

4 cups powdered sugar
1½ teaspoons vanilla

Brown the butter in a saucepan until delicately browned. Stir in the sugar and blend well. Add the cream and beat till smooth. Add the vanilla, spread on cake. Decorate with pecans.

Butter Creme Icing

½ cup butter
2 tablespoons whipping cream

1 16-oz. box powdered sugar
1 teaspoon vanilla

Beat the above to the desired consistency.

Peanut Butter Icing

½ cup cream-style peanut butter
¼ cup evaporated milk
1 teaspoon vanilla

3 cups powdered sugar
¼ cup butter

Combine all ingredients. Beat till smooth and thick.

Fastest Icing

1 large or 2 small boxes of vanilla instant pudding
1 pkg. dry whipped topping

Use ¼ cup less milk than pudding recipe requires. Beat the above and spread on cake. Add 1 can fruit cocktail, drained, sprinkled on cake.

Coconut Pecan Filling & Icing (Delicious)

1 can evaporated milk (12 oz.)
¼ cup butter
2 teaspoons vanilla
1 ½ cups pecans

1½ cups sugar
4 egg yolks
2½ cups coconut

Beat all ingredients (except pecans and coconut) together and cook and stir constantly for about 14 minutes until thickened. Remove from heat; add the pecans and coconut. Cool before spreading on cake.

Lillian's Mock Whipped Cream Icing 1950

Mix 1 cup milk with 2 heaping tablespoons cornstarch

Cook till thick, stirring constantly. Cool completely by beating with bowl in ice water. Cover with waxpaper.

Cream:
1 cup sugar
¼ cup shortening

1 stick margarine

Beat until light and fluffy. Add the cooked mixture and beat till creamy. Add any flavoring.

Coconut & Pecan Filling

1 large can evaporated milk
1 tablespoon vanilla

1½ cups sugar
3 large eggs

Cook the above till thick. Add:

2½ cups coconut

2¼ cups pecans

Cool and spread on cake.

Evelyn's Cream Filling

¾ cup sugar
¼ teaspoon salt
2 eggs beaten
1 teaspoon almond syrup

6 tablespoons flour
2 cups milk
2 teaspoons vanilla
1 tablespoon butter

Mix all together, then cook, stirring constantly till thick, enough for 3 layer cake. Spread between the layers.

Country Chocolate Icing

1 box (5.9-oz.) instant chocolate pudding
1 can (14-oz.) condensed milk
1 teaspoon butter nut extract
4 cups powdered sugar
½ stick margarine
8 oz. cream cheese
2 teaspoons vanilla

Combine all ingredients together. Beat for about 5 minutes.

Fluffy White Frosting

1 cup sugar
¼ teaspoon cream of tartar
2 large egg whites
⅓ cup water
dash of salt
2 teaspoons vanilla

In mixing bowl, beat egg whites till stiff peaks form. In saucepan put sugar, water, cream of tartar, salt and vanilla. Cook and stir till boiling. Then pour slowly over beaten egg whites. Beat on high speed of mixer about 7 minutes or till stiff peaks form.

Chocolate Glaze

1 cup powdered sugar
2 tablespoons milk
2 tablespoons baking cocoa
1 teaspoon vanilla

Stir all together till smooth. Spread on cake.

Fluffy Milky Smooth Icing

5 tablespoons all-purpose flour
1 cup milk

Beat the flour and milk till smooth. Bring to boil and cook till thick, about 2 minutes. Cover with plastic wrap and refrigerate till cool.

1 cup butter
2 ½ teaspoons vanilla
1 cup sugar

Cream butter, sugar and vanilla together. Add to milk mixture and beat for about 10 minutes or until fluffy.

Special Apple Streusel Topping

2 sticks butter
½ teaspoon cinnamon
1 cup pecans

1½ cups flour
3 cups sugar

Mix till crumbly. Spread half on cake. Peel and slice 2 apples very thin and arrange on top of cake; place last half of streusel on top of apples.

Vanilla Cream Cheese Icing

8 oz. cream cheese (softened)
5 cups powdered sugar
½ cup chop pecans to sprinkle on top of cake

1 stick butter
1 teaspoon vanilla

Beat the cream cheese and butter. Add the sugar and vanilla. Beat till smooth. Spread on cake. Sprinkle on pecans. Refrigerate.

Fluffy Frosting

1 tablespoon light corn syrup
¼ teaspoon cream of tartar
½ teaspoon salt
1 teaspoon vanilla

⅓ cup water
¾ cup sugar
1 egg white

Stir water, corn syrup, sugar, cream of tartar and salt together in a 2-quart saucepan. Bring the mixture to a full boil. Remove from heat. Beat egg white till frothy. Gradually pour hot syrup into egg white. Beat at high speed. Add vanilla. Beat until frosting stands in stiff peaks; frost cake.

Special Icing

1 3-oz. cream cheese
2 teaspoons milk

½ teaspoon vanilla
2½ cups powdered sugar

Mix all together and spread on cool cake.

A Hint: *Sprinkle cornstarch on cake before icing it, so the icing won't run.*

Whipped Cream Icing

2½ cups whipping cream
⅔ cup sifted powdered sugar

1 teaspoon vanilla

Beat whipping cream and vanilla at high speed of mixer until foamy. Gradually add powdered sugar, beating mixture until soft peaks form.

Evelyn's Pudding Frosting

1 3.4-oz. box instant vanilla pudding
1 teaspoon vanilla nut
1 sm. can crushed pineapple (drained)

1 16-oz. frozen whipped topping
1 teaspoon imitation butter
1 pkg. dry whipped topping

Beat all together and spread on cake.

Evelyn's Italian Cream Frosting

8 oz. cream cheese
1 cup pecans
1 teaspoon vanilla

1 box powdered sugar
1½ cups coconut

Add evaporated milk for spreading consistency. Stir in pecans and coconut. Spread on cake.

Gelatin Confetti Frosting

2 teaspoons unflavored gelatin
3 cups whipping cream (unwhipped)
2 teaspoons vanilla

3 tablespoons water
1 cup powdered sugar

Mix gelatin and water in saucepan. Set saucepan over low heat, stirring constantly till dissolved. Don't boil. Let cool. Combine other ingredients. Beat till thick.

How to Tint Coconut

Fill a jar half full of coconut, add 1 drop of desired food coloring add ¾ teaspoon water. Cover jar and shake till evenly spread.

Root Beer Frosting

3 cups powdered sugar
¼ cup butter

1 teaspoon root beer extract
3 tablespoons cream

Mix all ingredients till smooth.

Maple Flavor Icing

1 3-oz. cream cheese
3 cups powdered sugar
½ cup pecans
Dash salt

2 tablespoons butter
2 tablespoons corn syrup
1 teaspoon maple flavoring

Beat till smooth.

Chocolate Cream Cheese Icing

1 8-oz. cream cheese
2 teaspoons vanilla
⅓ cup French cocoa mix

½ stick butter
5 cups powdered sugar

Mix all together and beat till smooth.

Evelyn's Vanilla Cheesecake 50's

1½ lbs. cream cheese
2 tablespoons flour
2 teaspoons vanilla
1 cup crushed graham crackers

1 cup brown sugar
3 eggs (beat in 1 at a time)
1 stick margarine

Crush graham crackers with margarine. Spread on sides and bottom of cheesecake pan. Beat the cream cheese, flour, vanilla and brown sugar together. Beat in the eggs 1 at a time. Pour over the graham crackers and margarine. Bake at 350° for 50 minutes. Decorate with powdered sugar and pecans.

Evelyn's Fruit Cheese Cake

Spread 1 cup crushed graham crackers and 1 stick butter in pie plate. Mix:

1 8-oz. package cream cheese	1 can condensed milk
½ cup sugar	1 teaspoon vanilla
1 tablespoon lemon juice	1 pkg. dry whipped topping

Beat the above ingredients together for 5 minutes. Spread in pie plate over graham cracker crumbs and layer the following on the above:

2 cups fruit cocktail well drained	1 can of your favorite pie filling
1 cup pecans	2 pkgs. dry whipped topping
1 cup toasted coconut on top	

Top with cherry halves. Refrigerate till serving time.

Strawberry Cheesecake

Crust:

20 graham crackers (crushed)	1 stick butter
4 tablespoons powdered sugar	

Mix the above and press on sides and bottom of spring form pan.

1 can strawberry pie filling poured on top of crust

Filling:

4 large eggs	1 cup sugar
⅛ teaspoon salt	1 cup whipping cream
2 teaspoons vanilla	½ cup flour
2 8-oz. cream cheese	1 3-oz. box strawberry gelatin

Separate eggs and beat egg whites to soft peaks; set aside. Beat egg yolks, sugar, salt, cream, vanilla, flour, cheese and gelatin, till well blended. Pour on top of pie filling. Bake at 300° about 1 hour or till set. Decorate with fresh strawberries.

Best Blonde Brownies

2 cups flour	1 teaspoon baking powder
1 teaspoon salt	¼ teaspoon soda
1 cup pecans	1½ sticks butter
1 box brown sugar	2 eggs
2 teaspoons vanilla	

Beat all liquid ingredients. Beat in all dry sifted ingredients. Stir in pecans. Bake at 350° for 25 to 30 minutes.

Blonde Brownies

2 cups sifted flour
1½ teaspoons baking powder
1 teaspoon salt
1 cup chopped pecans

1 box brown sugar
3 large eggs beaten
2 teaspoons vanilla
1½ sticks margarine

Mix all together and pour into a greased 9 x 13-inch pan. Bake at 350° for 25 to 30 minutes.

Icing for brownies:
¼ cup baking cocoa
⅛ cup hot water
¼ cup sugar

1½ cups powdered sugar
1½ tablespoons butter

Beat till spreading consistency. Spread on brownies.

Brownie Caramel Sauce

1 cup whipping cream
3 tablespoons butter

½ cup brown sugar

Combine cream and sugar in saucepan, heat and stir till smooth. Stir in butter till melted. Serve warm or cold over brownies.

Brownies for a King

3 large eggs separated
6 tablespoons butter
3 tablespoons baking cocoa
1½ teaspoons baking powder
1 cup pecans

2 teaspoons vanilla
1½ cups sugar
3 tablespoons hot water
½ cup flour

Preheat oven to 350°. Whip egg whites till stiff, set aside. Mix rest of ingredients (except pecans) with mixer till smooth. Pour egg whites into batter and beat again. Stir in pecans. Pour batter into a greased 9-inch pan. Bake for 45 minutes.

Evelyn's Friendly Brownie Mix

Prepare ahead for a quick dessert. Or give as a gift.

Brownie mix:

1 cup plus 2 tablespoons all-purpose flour ⅔ cup brown sugar
⅔ cup sugar ½ teaspoon salt
1½ teaspoons baking powder 6 tablespoons baking cocoa

Put the flour in a quart jar. On top of the flour, layer the following in order given: brown sugar, salt, sugar, baking powder, cocoa. (Do not mix). Put on tight fitting lid. Place in cool place. Will last up to 5 months.

To prepare the brownies add the following:

4 large eggs 2 tablespoons water
¾ cup butter 2 teaspoons vanilla
1 teaspoon butter flavoring 1 cup pecans

Beat the eggs; add the butter and flavorings. Then add the brownie mix and stir in the pecans. Bake in 8 x 11½-inch glass pan lined with foil and greased. Bake at 350° for 35 to 40 minutes or until wooden pick inserted in center comes clean.

Texas Pecan Pineapple Cake

2 cups flour 2 cups sugar
2 ½ teaspoons baking powder 2 eggs
2 tablespoons butter 1 teaspoon vanilla
1 can 20-oz. undrained crushed pineapple
1 cup pecans

Mix all together, except stir in the pecans. Pour into greased 13 x 9 x 2-inch baking dish. Bake at 350° for 40 to 45 minutes till done. Cool.

Frosting:

2 cups powdered sugar 1 stick butter
1 8-oz. cream cheese 2 teaspoons vanilla

Beat till smooth. Frost cake; top with chopped pecans.

Canning & Freezing

Evelyn's Fruit Juice

2 boxes of oranges
6 pineapples
½ box peaches
1 box fruit color preserver or lemon juice to preserve color

1 box of apples
1 flat of strawberries
6 lbs. grapes

Put all this through a fruit and vegetable juicer. Put in 48-quart jars and freeze.

Hint: *Stand knife in jar when pouring hot jelly. Keeps jar from breaking.*

Mama's Tomato Preserves

2 cups tomatoes
Dash of cinnamon

1 cup sugar
Slice of lemon

Cook and stir constantly. Cook until it leaves a grove in the jelly while stirring. You may double or triple this recipe.

Mulberry Preserves

Wash mulberries, and put in pot with a small amount of water. Cook till soft, strain thru sieve to break up berries. Put 5½ cups mulberry juice and 1 box fruit pectin in pot; boil, stirring constantly. Let boil to a rolling boil that can't be stirred down. Quickly add 6½ cups sugar. Boil 1 minute, pour into jars and seal. Makes about 9 cups,

Peach Base Preserves

Wash peaches; peel, pit and put thru food processor. Put in pot with just enough water to cover bottom of pot. Let cook till peaches are tender, stirring constantly. Remove from heat and measure:

4 cups peaches
1 box fruit pectin

1 small box gelatin (any flavor)

Boil till you can't stir down the boil. Quickly add 5½ cups sugar; again boil till you can't stir it down. Boil 1 minute, put in jars and seal. Makes about 7 cups.

Garden Fresh Strawberry Preserves

Wash strawberries, remove stems and put thru food processor to chop up. Put in pot with just enough water to cover bottom of pot (if you don't have enough fresh berries, add some frozen ones). Cook till tender.

Add 5 cups strawberries and 1 box fruit pectin and boil till the boil can't be stirred down. Quickly add 7 cups sugar; again boil till it can't be stirred down. Cook for 1 minute; pour in jars and seal. Makes about 8 cups.

Evelyn's Jalapeño Jelly

Makes 3 ½ pints
1 lb. (combine) green, red and yellow bell peppers, seeds and veins removed, chopped fine
½ lb. jalapeño peppers (chop peppers with knife), seeds and veins removed (chopping peppers with food processor makes bubbles in jelly)
6 cups sugar
¾ cup 5 % white vinegar
½ cup red wine vinegar
2 boxes fruit pectin

Boil all ingredients except sugar, stirring constantly, add sugar. Bring to rolling boil and boil 1 minute. Pour into jars and seal.

Country Hot Jalapeños

Makes 1 pint
1 ¾ cup jalapeños (¼-inch sliced crossways, seeds removed)

All ingredients specified below put in a 1 cup measuring cup:
1 teaspoon salt
2 teaspoons olive oil
2 tablespoons red wine vinegar
2 tablespoons tarragon white wine vinegar
1 teaspoon balsamic vinegar
1 teaspoon walnut oil
¼ cup water

Fill rest of cup with 5% white vinegar. Boil the cup of brine; pour it over the jalapeños in the pint jar, and seal. Ready in about 2 weeks to enjoy.

Evelyn's Vegetable Juice

fresh tomatoes

fresh sweet pepper

fresh onion

fresh celery

fresh spaghetti squash

fresh jalapeño pepper

fresh garlic

fresh parsley

garlic and herb seasoning, Nature's Seasons and ginger

Remove seeds from peppers and squash. Blend with blender. Put tomatoes in blender, and put tomatoes thru sieve to remove seeds. Mix together; pour into canning jars and steam in pressure cooker 5 lbs. for 10 minutes.

Mama's Dill Pickles

3 quarts water

1 cup canning salt

1 qt. vinegar 5 %

9 qts. cucumbers

Put 2 grape leaves, 1 head of dill, 1 clove of garlic and 1 small red pepper in each jar, then wash and pack cucumbers in jars totaling 9 qts. Boil the water, vinegar and salt to boiling. Pour over the cucumbers, then seal.

Blue Ribbon Winner Bread & Butter Pickles

35 various sizes burpless cucumbers

¾ cup canning salt

8 large onions

Slice cukes very thin. Slice onions in food processor. Mix together with the salt. Let stand 3 hours, mixing often; drain very well.

Brine:

7½ cups vinegar

3 tablespoons mustard seed

⅓ cup rosemary vinegar

1½ tablespoons ginger

1 tablespoon dry red bell pepper

1 tablespoon soup and vegetable seasoning

7½ cups sugar

1½ teaspoons turmeric

1 tablespoon celery seed

3 tablespoons dry dill

Add cucumbers to brine and heat to boiling point, but don't boil. Fill jars. Wipe top of jars and seal. Makes about 8 pints.

Chili Sauce

10½ pounds tomatoes (chopped)
¾ pound sweet red peppers
1½ tablespoons salt

1½ cups onion
¾ pound sweet green peppers

Tie the following spices in cheese cloth:
1½ teaspoons mustard seed
2 bay leafs
1½ tablespoons celery seed

¾ teaspoon whole spice
¾ teaspoon whole cloves

Add:
2½ cups white vinegar

¾ cup sugar

In large pot put the chopped vegetables and tied spices and salt. On medium heat cook till thickened, stirring constantly. Remove tied spice. Add vinegar and sugar cook on medium heat till mixture is a thick sauce. Put in jars and seal.

Blue Ribbon Tomato Soup

16 pounds of tomatoes (peeled and seeds extracted)
7 medium onions (peeled and chunked)
6 medium bell peppers (chopped large pieces)
2 hot peppers (cut in half)
4 stalks celery (cut in 3-inch lengths)
1 cup fresh parsley
6 bay leafs
1 stick butter
½ cup sugar
1½ tablespoons salt
1 teaspoon white pepper

Put all together in large pot (except butter and sugar) and cook for 1 hour, stirring often. Then strain, remove the celery and bay leaf (discard). The peppers, onions and parsley put in blender till smooth. Put back into pot; add the butter and sugar. Boil for 15 minutes. Put in jars and seal. Makes about 9 pints.

Ranch Salsa Sauce

Weighed after all vegetables were prepared:

10 lbs. tomatoes	1½ lbs. bell pepper
1¾ lbs. onions	1½ lbs. cucumbers
1½ lbs. zucchini squash	1½ lbs. yellow squash
1 oz. garlic	1 oz. jalapeño pepper

Spices follow:

1 tablespoon garlic salt	1 tablespoon pinch of herbs
1 tablespoon garlic and herb	1 teaspoon cumin
1 tablespoon mesquite seasoning	5 tablespoons salt
1 tablespoon frijoles seasoning	1 teaspoon chili powder
1 tablespoon cilantro	1 teaspoon oregano
1 cup white corn syrup	1 pkg. (1.25 oz.) taco seasoning

Dice all vegetables. Add the spices. Put in a 20-qt. stainless pot. Simmer for 2 hours, on medium heat. Put in jars; pressure cook for 10 minutes on 5 lbs.

Oven Tomatoes

Peel tomatoes. Put in pint jars. Place just the lids on, put in oven at 250° for 75 minutes. Let cool overnight. Put on rings and screw down.

Hotter than Fire Sauce

3 tablespoons grapeseed garlic and parsley oil

2 tablespoons olive oil	2 cups chopped onion

Sauté the above for about 5 minutes.

10 cups canned tomatoes	3 teaspoons dried garlic
1 tablespoon dried cilantro	1 teaspoon ginger
2 teaspoons jalapeño salt	½ cup sugar
¼ cup hot sauce	1 tablespoon garlic and herb
¼ cup red vinegar	½ cup tarragon vinegar
⅓ cup chopped chili petin peppers	1 tablespoon jalapeño seasoning
2 tablespoons dried jalapeño peppers	
2 tablespoons Creole and Cajun seasoning	
4 cups chopped jalapeño peppers with seed	

Mix the above in a large pot and cook for about 1½ hours on medium heat, stirring frequently. Put in sterilized jars and seal. Put in hot water bath 30 minutes.

Pear Relish

12 large pears	12 medium onions
12 medium bell peppers	2 tablespoons salt
2 cups sugar	2 cups vinegar
2 small jars mustard	3 jalapeños

Grind the above together. Cook, stirring constantly, for about 20 minutes. Put in jars and seal.

Evelyn's Jalapeño Supreme

1 gallon jalapeños cut in half and seeds removed.

Put in a gallon jar. Cover jalapeños with the following vinegars:

¼ cup rosemary vinegar
½ cup red wine vinegar (use ¼ cup each of 2 different brands)
¼ cup white wine vinegar
¼ cup tarragon wine vinegar
rest is regular 5% vinegar

Put a lid on the jar and stand on counter top for 3 weeks. Get your small jars and lids ready. Then drain peppers in colander very well. Put peppers in pan and put about 4 cups of sugar on top of peppers and coat peppers with the sugar, very quickly. Put in the small jars before the sugar starts to dissolve. Fill jar with tap water. Put on lid and ring. No need to seal.

Freezing Fresh Peaches
(No sugar)

Put fresh peaches in boiling water, then in ice water for a fast cool off, peel and pit. Put in water with fruit preserver. I need 2½ to 3 cups of peaches for most recipes. Take a 3-lb. margarine container and fill with peaches to about ⅔ full, then sprinkle some fruit preserver on top. Add water. Pour it into a quart plastic bag and squeeze all the air out and seal it, put it in the freezer. Then vacuum seal the bags.

Freezing Sweet Corn

Shuck corn and remove corn silks. Cut corn off cob or freeze whole ears. Put corn in plastic bags and freeze. Put in seal bags and seal with vacuum sealer.

Freezing Tomato Puree

Cut up tomatoes, put in blender and blend till completely pureed. Pour into strainer and take a water glass and press puree through strainer to remove seeds. Put in plastic bags, the amount you will use at 1 time. I always put 1 cup in each bag. Seal and freeze.

Note: *Canning: 18 lbs. tomatoes = 25 cups juice*

Freezing Fresh Onions

Chop or slice onions; put in plastic bags and freeze.

Freezing Fresh Irish Potatoes

Scrape skins off. Put potatoes in plastic bags. Fill with water, squeeze air out. Seal. Freeze. Vacuum seal bags.

Dehydrated Bell Peppers

Clean and slice peppers with food processor (with the large slicer blade) and put in dehydrator.

Freezing Turnips

Peel turnips and cut in desired pieces. Blanch in boiling water for 3 minutes; drain and put in ice water to cool. Put in plastic bags. Squeeze out air. Seal and freeze. Then vacuum seal.

Red Bell Pepper

Buy red peppers on sale, cut in 4 pieces and clean seeds out. Put in plastic bags, seal and freeze. When needed, run hot water on them, peel and use.

Homemade Sauerkraut

Wash jars and have jars ready for a quick fill. Wash cabbage. Cut heads in half, remove core and shred very thin. Put in large container. To 20 to 25 pounds add 8 oz. salt.

Mix thoroughly. Pack jars quickly (*Reason: The last of your cabbage will wilt with the salt and the last fills will be packed to tight in the jars*). Leave about 2 inches of space in jar when all jars are filled.

Pour boiling water into jar; work water down with a knife so there are no air bubbles in jar. Clean top of jar. Place lid and ring and tighten.

Put jars in old ice chest or some leak-proof container. It will ferment for about 3 weeks, and will drain. And the smell is strong. After that, wash jars. And enjoy your labor.

Cookies, Bars & Candy

Evelyn's Crunchy Candy Cookies # 2

3 cups flour
½ teaspoons salt
1 cup sugar
3 large eggs
2 teaspoons vanilla
11.5 oz. real milk chocolate chips
12 oz. white chocolate chips
3 teaspoons baking powder
1 cup (2 sticks) butter
1 cup brown sugar
2 teaspoons vanilla nut extract
1 teaspoon almond extract
4 cups pecans
1 tablespoon French vanilla cocoa mix
¼ cup coconut syrup or ¼ cup corn syrup with coconut extract
14 oz. chocolate candy with crisped rice (it's a candy bar) (chopped up)

Combine butter, sugars, eggs, flavorings, cocoa mix and syrup. Beat till very creamy. Mix flour, baking powder and salt. Add to the creamy mixture, 3 different times, beating well. Stir in the chocolates and pecans. Drop on greased cookie sheet with a teaspoon. Bake at 350° for about 10 minutes or till cookie edges are tan.

Meringue Cookies (Sandra)

3 large egg whites
¼ teaspoon salt
1 cup pecans
1 cup sugar
2 teaspoons vanilla

Preheat oven to 300°. Blend egg whites, sugar, salt and vanilla in top of double boiler; place over boiling water and beat with mixer till stiff peaks form. Drop by teaspoonful on cookie sheet. Bake for 12 or 15 minutes. Remove from cookie sheet immediately.

Giant Cocoa Meringue Cookies

4 large egg whites
1 box powdered sugar
¼ cup baking cocoa
⅛ teaspoon salt
2 teaspoons vanilla
1 cup pecans

Beat egg whites till foamy; gradually add sugar. Beat on high speed till meringue forms soft peaks. Beat in vanilla and cocoa. Stir in pecans. On a wax paper-lined cookie sheet, drop dough by tablespoon. Bake at 325° for 10 minutes or till tops of cookies are firm and centers are moist. Let completely cool before removing from cookie sheet.

Etherine's Cookie Kisses

3 egg whites
½ teaspoon cream of tartar
½ cup coconut

1 cup sugar
1 teaspoon vanilla

Beat first 4 ingredients till stiff; stir in coconut. Bake at 300° for 25 minutes till golden brown. *Optional:* 2 tablespoons baking cocoa, ¾ cup pecans.

Texas Oatmeal Cookies

3 cups flour
½ teaspoon salt
½ cup butter (1 stick)
1 cup sugar
2 teaspoons vanilla
⅔ cup milk
2 cups pecans
2 cups white chocolate chips
¼ cup coconut syrup or corn syrup with coconut flavoring

2 teaspoons baking powder
1 cup shortening
1 cup brown sugar
4 large eggs
1 teaspoon vanilla nut extract
6 cups oatmeal
¼ cup coconut

Beat together the shortening, butter, eggs, sugars, flavorings, about half of the milk. Mix the flour, baking powder and salt together. Add the flour mixture to the shortening mixture. Add the other half of the milk and beat till creamy. Stir in the coconut and pecans. Drop on greased cookie sheet with teaspoon. Bake at 375° for about 12 minutes or till tan around the edges.

Best Ever Melting Moments Cookies

1 cup butter
2 teaspoons almond extract
2 cups flour
1 cup pecans

1 cup powdered sugar
½ teaspoon salt
2 teaspoons baking powder

Cream together butter, sugar and almond and beat till very creamy and fluffy. Add the flour, baking powder and salt. Beat well. Stir in pecans. Place on un-greased cookie sheet with teaspoon and flatten with bottom of water glass. Bake at 350° till edge of cookies are tan, about 10 minutes.

The Best Rice Krispie Cookies

3½ cups flour
1 teaspoon salt

1½ teaspoons baking powder
½ teaspoon cinnamon

Mix the 4 above ingredients together. Set aside. Beat the following together till very creamy:

½ cup milk
2 teaspoons maple flavoring
2 cups sugar

2 eggs
1 cup (solid) shortening (no oil)
½ cup brown sugar

Add the flour mixture to the above and beat till very smooth. Mix the 3 following ingredients. Together and stir into the above.

4 cups chopped pecans
4 cups Rice Krispies

¾ cup white chocolate chips

Drop by teaspoonful on greased cookie sheet. Bake at 350° for 15 minutes or till cookies are tan around edge.

Grandmo's Pecan Cookies 20's

1 cup butter
1 teaspoon water
2 cups flour

⅓ cup brown sugar (packed)
1 teaspoon vanilla
1 cup pecans

Bake at 350° till golden color.

Evelyn's Maple Cookies

1 ¾ cups flour
½ teaspoon salt
¼ cup milk
2 large eggs beaten
1 cup sugar
1 cup pecans

1 teaspoon baking powder
½ teaspoon cinnamon
1 teaspoon maple flavoring
1 stick butter
1 cup Rice Krispies

Cream sugar and butter till very fluffy. Add all the rest of ingredients except Rice Krispies and pecans; stir in. Bake at 350° for about 15 minutes or till golden brown edges.

Evelyn's Ranger Cookies 50's

1 cup shortening
1 cup sugar
2 cups cornflakes (crushed)
2 cups flour
½ teaspoon salt
2 teaspoons vanilla

1 cup brown sugar (packed)
2 large eggs
2 cups oatmeal
3 teaspoons baking powder
1 cup coconut
1 cup pecans

Mix till smooth, stir in pecans and cornflakes. Drop by spoonfuls on greased cookie sheet. Bake at 350° till light brown. Makes about 6 dozen.

Spritz-zy Cookies

1 cup butter
1½ cups sugar
2 teaspoons vanilla
4½ cups flour
½ teaspoon salt

½ cup solid shortening
2 large eggs
2 teaspoons vanilla nut extract
1 teaspoon baking powder

Mix flour, baking powder and salt together. Combine butter, shortening, eggs, sugar and extracts; beat till fluffy. Add flour mixture alternately, beating after each addition. Put dough in cookie press and press out on ungreased cookie sheet. Bake at 375° for about 8 minutes or till cookies are tan around edges.

Cookie variations

Eggnog cookies:
Add 1 teaspoon nutmeg

Chocolate almond cookies:
Add 1½ teaspoon almond and 3 tablespoons French vanilla cocoa mix

Maple flavor cookies:
Add 1 tablespoon maple flavoring and omit the vanillas

Haystack Macaroon Cookies 50's

2 large egg whites
1 teaspoon vanilla
½ cup pecans

1 cup sugar
½ cup coconut
2 cups crisp cornflakes

Beat egg whites until stiff and dry; fold in sugar gradually. Add vanilla, coconut, pecans and cornflakes. Drop by teaspoonful on well-greased baking sheet. Bake at 375° for about 8 minutes. When cool store in airtight jar.

Helen's Variety Cookies 50's

6 tablespoons shortening
1 tablespoon milk
1 teaspoon vanilla
1½ teaspoons baking powder

¾ cup sugar
1 large egg
2 cups flour
⅛ teaspoon salt

Cream shortening and sugar. Add egg, milk, vanilla. Sift flour, salt and baking powder together; mix well. Roll out thin and cut with cookie cutter. Bake on greased sheets. Bake at 350° for 8 to 10 minutes.

For pecan cookies: add ½ cup pecans

For chocolate chip: add ⅔ cup chocolate chips

For spice: add 1 teaspoon cinnamon, ¼ teaspoon cloves, ¼ teaspoon nutmeg

For cocoa cookies: add ¼ cup cocoa and 2 tablespoons milk

Macaroons Cookies 1966

4 egg whites (beaten to stiff peaks)
1 cup coconut
4 cups cornflakes crushed

1¼ cups sugar
½ cup pecans
2 teaspoons vanilla

Drop by teaspoonful on ungreased cookie sheet. Bake at 325° for about 10 minutes.

Persimmon Cookies

½ cup butter
1 egg
2 cups flour
1 cup pecans
½ teaspoon of each: cinnamon, cloves and nutmeg

1 cup sugar
1 cup pulp from persimmon
1 teaspoon soda
Raisins or dates optional

Drop by spoonfuls on greased cookie sheet. Bake at 350° for 12 to 15 minutes. Makes 4 dozen.

Lillian's Sour Cream Cookies 50's

1 cup sugar   ½ cup butter

Cream together.

Add 2 eggs and beat together till smooth.

½ cup sour cream   2 cups flour
1 teaspoon soda   ¼ teaspoon salt
1 cup quick oatmeal   1 cup coconut
1 cup dates   1 cup pecans
1 teaspoon vanilla

Mix all together. Stir in pecans. Drop on greased cookie sheet. Bake at 375° for about 12 minutes.

Cookie Icing

¼ cup melted butter   2 cups powdered sugar
1 tablespoon milk

Cream together till smooth. Spread on cookies.

Best Thumbprint Cookies

¼ cup butter   ¼ cup shortening
1 cup brown sugar   1 large egg
1 teaspoon vanilla   1 cup flour
¼ teaspoon salt   ½ teaspoon baking powder
¾ cup pecans

Drop by tablespoons on ungreased cookie sheet. Press thumb in center. Bake at 350° for 10 minutes. Makes 3 dozen. When cool, put jalapeño jelly or your favorite jelly in thumbprint.

Mama's Butterscotch Cookies 40's

2 cups brown sugar   1 cup butter
2 large eggs   1 teaspoon baking powder
3 cups flour   1 cup pecans
1 teaspoon vanilla

Mix and roll dough. Let stand all night in refrigerator. In morning, slice and bake at 350° for 10 minutes.

Ultimate Sugar Cookies

1¼ cups sugar
2 large eggs
1 tablespoon vanilla
¾ teaspoon baking powder

1 cup shortening
¼ cup light corn syrup
3¼ cups flour
½ teaspoon salt

Beat sugar and shortening till fluffy. Add rest of ingredients. Roll dough into ¼-inch thickness and cut out. Bake at 375° for 5 to 7 minutes. Makes 3½ dozen.

Jalapeño Filled Cookies

1	2	3	4	times the recipe
1	1½	2	2½	cups butter
½	¾	1	1¼	cups vegetable shortening
1½	2¼	3	3¾	cups sugar
4	6	8	10	large eggs
4½	6¾	9	11¼	cups flour
½	¾	1	1¼	teaspoons baking powder
½	¾	1	1¼	teaspoons salt
3	4	5	6	teaspoons vanilla
1	2	3	4	tablespoons corn syrup
1	2	3	4	teaspoons almond syrup
1	2	3	4	teaspoons butter rum syrup

Beat eggs sugar, butter, shortening and flavorings. Sift flour, baking powder and salt. Beat into batter. Put in cookie press and press out on greased cookie sheet. Make dent in center of cookie about the size of a nickel. Bake at 375° for about 7 or 8 minutes. Fill centers with jalapeño jelly at serving time.

Forgotten Oatmeal & Apple Cookies

¾ cup shortening
1 large egg
1½ teaspoons vanilla
½ teaspoon salt
¼ teaspoon nutmeg
1 cup diced apples

1¼ cups brown sugar
¼ cup milk
1¼ teaspoons cinnamon
¼ teaspoon baking powder
3 cups oatmeal
1 cup pecans

Grease cookie sheet. Drop by tablespoon about 2 inches apart on cookie sheet. Bake at 375° for 13 minutes. Makes 2½ dozen.

Evelyn's Crunch Candy Cookies

3 cups flour
½ teaspoon salt
1 cup sugar
1 cup brown sugar
1 teaspoon vanilla nut
21 oz. Buncha Crunch chocolate candy or chocolate chips

3 teaspoons baking powder
1 cup (2 sticks) butter
3 large eggs
1 teaspoon vanilla
3 cups pecans

Mix all together. Drop by teaspoon on greased cookie sheet. Bake at 375° for 10 minutes or till done.

Old Timer Wedding Cookies

1 stick butter
3 oz. cream cheese
2 teaspoons vanilla
1 cup pecans

1 cup sugar
½ teaspoon almond extract
1 cup flour

Preheat oven 350°. Blend sugar, butter and cheese. Beat till fluffy. Beat in extracts and flour. Stir in pecans. Roll dough into 1-inch balls and flatten. Place on ungreased cookie sheet. Bake about 16 minutes or till lightly brown. Sprinkle powdered sugar on top of cookies.

Grandma's Cream Puffs

½ cup butter
1 cup boiling water

4 large eggs
1 cup flour

Put butter and water in pot and boil. Add flour and beat. Cook till edges don't stick to pot, constantly stirring. Cool. Beat in eggs one at a time till smooth. Drop by spoonful on greased cookie sheet. Pile the mixture slightly in center. Bake at 350° for about 40 minutes.

Mix all ingredients till smooth. Cook for 15 minutes on medium heat. Cool. Make slit in top of cream puff and fill with filling.

Filling: 2 cups milk, ½ cup flour, 1 cup sugar, 2 large eggs, 2 teaspoons vanilla and ⅛ teaspoon salt. Put all 6 ingredients in blender and blend. Pour into pot, and cook till thick, about 15 minutes. Cool. Fill cream puffs.

Optional Chocolate Filling:
1¼ cups sugar
½ teaspoon salt
2¼ cups milk
3 tablespoons baking cocoa

½ cup + 1 tablespoon flour
3 large eggs
2 teaspoons vanilla

Evelyn's Delicious 2002 Cookies

3 large eggs
1 cup brown sugar
1 teaspoon vanilla nut
3 cups flour
½ teaspoon salt
½ cup coconut
3 cups pecans
1 cup white chocolate chips
3 heaping teaspoons French vanilla cocoa mix

1 cup sugar
2 teaspoons vanilla
1 teaspoon butter pecan
3 teaspoons baking powder
1 cup (2 sticks) butter
1 cup rice krispies
1 cup dark chocolate chips

Beat eggs and sugars for about 5 minutes with electric mixer. Put in butter and flavorings. Beat on high speed for 5 minutes. Mix flour, baking powder, salt and cocoa powder. Add to batter; beat 3 minutes. Mix together chocolate chips, coconut, rice krispies and pecans. Stir into batter.

Drop by tablespoon on greased cookie sheet. Bake at 350° for about 10 minutes or till brown edges. Or bake convection oven at 325° for about 10 minutes or brown edges. Makes 96 cookies.

Pecan Coconut Bars

½ cup butter   2 cups brown sugar packed

Beat the above till smooth.

2 eggs
2 teaspoons baking powder
1½ teaspoons vanilla
1 tablespoon white corn syrup

2 cups flour
¼ teaspoon salt
1 teaspoon vanilla nut

Beat the above into the sugar and butter. Stir in:

1 cup pecans   1 cup coconut

Pour and spread batter with spoon into a 13 x 9 x 2-inch greased pan. Bake at 350° for 30 minutes.

Pecan Praline Candy

1 lb. brown sugar
2 tablespoons butter
Pinch salt

1 can condensed milk
1 tablespoon vanilla
2 cups pecans

Boil sugar and milk until it forms a soft ball. Remove from heat; add butter, vanilla, salt and pecans. Beat till creamy. Drop on waxed paper by spoonful. Makes 35.

Country Pecan Pie Bars

2 cups flour   ½ cup sugar
⅛ teaspoon salt   ¾ cup butter

Combine the 4 above ingredients with a pastry blender, until mixture resembles very fine crumbs. Press mixture evenly into a greased 13 x 9-inch pan; press crumb mixture firmly in pan. Bake at 350° for 18 to 22 minutes or till lightly brown.

Topping:
1 cup brown sugar   1 cup white corn syrup
½ cup butter   4 eggs lightly beaten
2 cups pecans   2 teaspoons vanilla

Bring to a boil the sugar, corn syrup and butter in a saucepan. Stirring gently, remove from heat. Stir one-fourth of the hot mixture into the beaten eggs, add to remaining hot mixture. Stir in pecans and vanilla; pour filling over crust. Bake at 350° for 35 to 38 minutes or until set. Cool completely and cut into bars. Makes about 16.

Pecan Pie Surprise Bars 50's

1 box yellow cake mix (reserve ⅔ cup cake mix)
½ cup butter   1 egg

Grease 13 x 9-inch pan. Mix the above till crumbly and press into pan. Bake at 350° for 15 to 20 minutes until light brown.

Filling:
⅔ cup cake mix   ½ cup brown sugar
3 large eggs   1½ cups corn syrup
2 teaspoons vanilla   1 cup pecans

Prepare filling and pour over baked crust. Sprinkle with pecans. Bake at 350° for 30 to 35 minutes.

Auntie's Marshmallow Bars 50's

¼ cup butter   2 teaspoons vanilla
5 cups Rice Krispies   1 cup pecans
40 large marshmallows or 4 cups miniature marshmallows

Put rice krispies in greased pan (large enough to stir mixture in). Melt butter and marshmallows till smooth. Pour over rice krispies and mix till Rice Krispies are coated. Press mixture evenly into a buttered 13 x 2 x 22-inch pan. When cool, cut in bars.

Auntie's Pecan Bars 50's

1 lb. brown sugar   4 eggs slightly beaten

Beat eggs in double boiler with brown sugar; cook until sugar is melted. Cool. Add:

2 cups chopped pecans   1 teaspoon vanilla
2 cups flour sifted twice   2 teaspoons baking powder

Spread in a large greased sheet pan. Bake at 350° for 25 to 30 minutes. Cut in bars.

Betty's Praline Bars 50's

1 box brown sugar   2 cups biscuit and pancake mix
4 large eggs   1 cup pecans

Mix all ingredients very well and pour into a greased 5½ x 10½ x 2-inch pan. Preheat oven to 350°. Bake about 30 to 40 minutes. Cool, cut in bars.

Evelyn's Chocolate Pecans Diamonds 1987

Crust:
¾ cup butter   ½ cup powdered sugar
½ teaspoon salt   2 cups flour

Mix and press in bottom of greased jelly roll pan. Preheat oven to 375°. Reduce oven temp. to 350°, bake for 20 minutes.

Filling:
4 eggs   1½ cups brown sugar
3 cups pecans   3 tablespoons baking cocoa
2 teaspoons vanilla   ½ teaspoon salt

Blend eggs, sugar and etc. together. Pour over hot crust. Bake at 350° for 20 minutes. When cool, cut into strips. Freezes easily.

Round Peanut Candy

3¼ cups sugar
1 cup corn syrup
¼ teaspoon red food coloring
Pinch of salt

1 cup water
1 lb. raw peanuts
½ stick butter

Bring sugar, water, syrup to a boil. Add peanuts and coloring; cook until hard ball stage. Remove from heat, add butter and salt. Beat until mixture is too thick to beat. Pour onto greased cookie sheet. Break into pieces when cool.

Easy "Toffee" Candy

Line a 15 x 10 x 1-inch jelly roll pan with foil, spray with nonstick spray. Melt ¼ cup butter in pan. Arrange 40 saltine crackers over butter. Break crackers to fit empty spaces. Melt 1 cup butter; add 1 cup brown sugar. Bring to boil over medium heat. Reduce heat to low cook, stirring occasionally for 2 minutes. Remove from heat. Stir in 1 can of condensed milk. Pour over crackers. Bake at 425° for 10 to 12 minutes or until mixture is bubbly and slightly darkened. Remove from oven. Cool for 1 minute.

Sprinkle with 1½ cups chocolate morsels. Let stand 5 minutes, until morsels are shiny. Spread evenly. Sprinkle with 1 cup pecans. Cool about 30 minutes until chocolate is set. Remove foil; cut in pieces.

Dairy Fudge Candy

1 lb. butter
4 lbs. powdered sugar
1 cup baking cocoa

1 lb. Velveeta cheese
1 tablespoon vanilla
2 cups pecans

Melt butter and cheese. Sift sugar and cocoa in large bowl. Add vanilla, butter, cheese and pecans to sugar mixture. Pour into greased pan. Let set and cut into squares.

Spiced Pecans

1 cup sugar
⅓ cup evaporated milk
1 teaspoon vanilla

½ teaspoon cinnamon
1½ cups pecans

Mix sugar and cinnamon. Stir in milk; cook to soft ball stage. Add pecans and vanilla; stir until well coated. Pour onto wax paper-lined pan and separate.

Quick Delights Candy 50's

1½ boxes powdered sugar
1 stick butter
1 can condensed milk

1 cup coconut flakes
2 to 3 cups pecans

Mix ingredients together. Chill. Roll into 1-inch balls. Chill. In double boiler, melt 12-oz. pkg. chocolate chips and ¼ lb. paraffin. Dip the balls in the chocolate mixture and place on waxed paper to harden.

Evelyn's Delicious Praline Candy

5 cups brown sugar
2 cans condensed milk
1 tablespoon vanilla
1 cup sweet potatoes (cooked and mashed)
1 cup pumpkin (cooked and mashed)
6 cups pecans

1 cup sugar
4 tablespoons butter
1 teaspoon salt

1. Cook potatoes and pumpkin separately, in a small amount of water. When they are very tender, drain water. Can do 1 or 2 days before, then refrigerate.
2. Put milk, butter, salt, pumpkin, sweet potatoes and vanilla in a blender; blend till smooth. Heat pecans in pan in oven till warm.
3. In saucepan put the blended mixture and sugars; stir constantly. Cook to 230°, soft ball stage. Remove from heat, add pecans and stir till creamy. Drop on foil that has been sprayed with nonstick spray. When cold, wrap each one in clear wrap.

Cheerios or Cheetos Toffee

1 cup sugar   1 cup butter

Heat to boiling, stirring constantly over medium heat, until mixture becomes light brown and thickened, about 8 to 10 minutes. Remove from heat.

Stir in 2½ cups Cheerios or Cheetos until well coated, turn onto ungreased baking sheet. Spread mixture. Cool; break into pieces.

Vanilla Marshmallows

½ cup of each cornstarch and powdered sugar
2 cups sugar   1⅓ cups hot water
¼ cup light corn syrup   ¼ teaspoon salt
½ cup cold water   2 teaspoons vanilla
3 envelopes unflavored gelatin = 2 tablespoons
6 large egg whites   ½ teaspoon cream of tartar

1. Lightly butter a 13 x 9 x 2-inch baking pan; coat with 2 tablespoons of cornstarch and powdered sugar mixture.
2. Mix sugar, hot water, corn syrup and salt; boil till reaches 260° (15 to 20 minutes).
3. Pour cold water and gelatin together; heat till gelatin dissolves. Stir in vanilla; keep warm.
4. Before syrup reaches 260° start beating egg whites and cream of tartar. Beat till billowy peaks form, slowly adding hot syrup in a thin stream. Pour in warm gelatin. Beat 10 minutes, until mixture is cool and fluffy.
5. Turn out into prepared pan smooth surface. Let stand till cool in dry place for 3 hours or until set.
6. Loosen edges of mixture with knife, cut with wet knife, toss each cube in cornstarch and powdered sugar mixture. Let dry 1 hour. Makes 72.

The 1950's Cocoa Fudge

⅔ cup baking cocoa   ⅛ teaspoon salt
¼ cup butter   3 cups sugar
1½ cups milk   2 teaspoons vanilla
1 cup pecans

Combine cocoa, sugar and salt in large saucepan. Add milk gradually; mix thoroughly. Bring to a bubbly boil on high heat, stirring continuously. Reduce heat to medium and continue to boil the mixture without stirring until it reaches a temp. of 232°. Remove saucepan from heat; add butter, vanilla and pecans to mixture. Cool some while stirring, and pour in a greased 8 x 8 x 2-inch pan.

Desserts, Cobblers,
Ice Cream & Pies

Evelyn's Rainbow Tulip Dessert

1 sm. box strawberry gelatin, make according to directions
1 sm. box tropical fruit gelatin, make according to directions
1 sm. box pistachio instant pudding, make according to directions
Frozen whipped topping   Cherries

Use 5 long-stem 1-cup capacity glasses. Lean them in a bowl in the refrigerator. Mix the strawberry gelatin and pour in the leaning glasses. Make sure they lean enough so you cover ½ of the bottom of the glass. The gelatin should be from the top of the glass to the half of the glass bottom.

Let set about 1½ hours. Make the other box of gelatin an hour later and stand in refrigerator. It can cool. After the 1½ hours of setting, turn your glasses, and pour in the 2nd box of gelatin from top of glass to ½ of the bottom. Let set another 1½ hours or till really set. Now stand glasses up.

Mix the pudding and pour into the glasses. You have a beautiful tulip effect. Let set 30 minutes. Use a cake decorator and pipe frozen whipped topping on top. Place a cherry on top of each glass. Now sit back and listen to the comments!

Texas Best Gelatin and Pineapple Dessert

1 cup flour   1 cup pecans chopped
1 stick margarine or butter   ½ cup brown sugar

Mix the above. Spread in 8 x 12 -inch baking dish that has been sprayed with nonstick spray. Bake at 400° for 8 minutes.

1 20-oz. can crushed pineapple (drain and save juice)

Boil pineapple juice and dissolve.

13¼-oz. strawberry gelatin. Stir till dissolved, then cool.

Beat with electric mixer:

1 8-oz. cream cheese   ⅔ cup condensed milk
½ cup sugar

Beat in the pineapple and gelatin. Pour over the baked crust. Put in refrigerator till gelatin sets.

Ice Cream Gelatin Dessert

Mix 1 small or 1 large box any flavor gelatin with 1 cup or 2 cups hot water to melt gelatin. Add 1 cup or 2 cups vanilla ice cream instead of cold water. Serve in dessert bowls. Top with frozen topping.

Apple Chewy Pecan Dessert

¾ cup flour
1½ teaspoons baking powder
1 teaspoon vanilla
½ cup pecans

¾ cup sugar
1 large egg beaten
1 cup chopped apples

Bake in ungreased pie pan. Bake at 300° for 1 hour.

Country Best Peach Crisp Dessert

Preheat oven to 375°. Spray a 10½ x 15-inch baking dish with nonstick spray.

1 can condensed milk
1½ cups flour
2 teaspoons vanilla

8 cups fresh peaches (sliced)
2 cups sugar

Mix the above and spread mixture in baking dish.

Topping:
3 cups chopped pecans
2½ cups brown sugar
1 teaspoon cinnamon
2 sticks butter

1½ cups cornflakes (crushed)
2 cups flour
2 tablespoons vanilla
2 teaspoons butternut extract

Mix the topping and sprinkle on top of the peach mixture. Bake approximately 40 minutes.

Peach Crisp Dessert

4 cups peaches (juice drained; if you are using
    fresh peaches sprinkle with lemon juice)
¾ cup flour   1 cup sugar

Mix and put the above mixture in a greased 13 x 9-inch pan.

Topping:
1¼ cups brown sugar
1 teaspoon cinnamon
½ cup crushed cornflakes

1 cup flour
6 tablespoons butter
3 cups pecans

Bake at 375° for 30 minutes.

Cocktail Rice Pudding

1 15¼-oz. can fruit cocktail (drain and save juice)
3 cups milk and saved juice (combined)
1 4.6-oz. box vanilla cook-and-serve pudding
¼ cup sugar   1¼ cups instant rice
2 teaspoons vanilla

In a saucepan combine the milk, juice, pudding, sugar and vanilla. Cook on medium heat, stirring constantly, till almost boiling. Add rice and bring to boil. Boil for about 3 minutes, stirring constantly. Remove from heat, add fruit cocktail. Put in Pyrex bowl, cover with glass lid. When cool, put in refrigerator to get cold. Serve and enjoy.

Layered Delight Dessert 50's

1 cup flour   1 cup pecans
1 stick butter

Mix together and press into a greased 9 x 13-inch pan. Bake at 350° till light brown.

2nd layer:
8 oz. cream cheese   1 cup powdered sugar
8 oz. frozen whipped topping

3rd layer:
2 boxes vanilla instant pudding   3 cups milk

Beat till thick. Cool.

4th layer:
Top with frozen whipped topping.

Country Crusty Fruit Gelatin

Preheat oven to 400°

1 cup flour
1 stick butter

1 cup pecans (chopped)
¾ cup brown sugar

Mix the above till crumbly. Press in a greased 9 x 12-inch pan. Bake the above for 8 minutes. Cool the above.

3 cups fruit (cut up and drain; save juice), fruit cocktail, peaches or pears

Boil 1¼ cups fruit juice (your preference) add 1 (3-oz.) box gelatin (strawberry or any flavor). Mix juice and gelatin together. Cook till dissolved; cool.

Put in a separate mixing bowl and beat together:

1 8-oz. cream cheese
½ cup sugar

⅔ cup condensed milk

Beat till thoroughly mixed.

Fold the fruit into the cream cheese mixture and stir in the gelatin. Pour over the baked ingredients. Put in refrigerator and let set about 3 hours. May serve it after 3 hours, or freeze it for later use.

Evelyn's Gelatin Supreme Dessert

1 9-inch cake layer diced up, put in clear glass bowl

Mix the following together:

1 3-oz. box strawberry gelatin
1 15-oz. can fruit cocktail (drain and save)
1 cup of water and saved fruit cocktail juice combined

1 cup hot water

Pour the above over the cake. Press the cake into the liquid and refrigerate till set (about 1½ hours).

2nd layer:
1 3⅛-oz. vanilla instant pudding
2 cups cold milk

1 envelope dry whipped topping
2 teaspoons vanilla

Beat together and pour over gelatin. Let it sit about 30 minutes.

3rd layer:
1 3⅛-oz. pistachio instant pudding
⅛ cup milk

16 oz. frozen whipped topping
2 teaspoons vanilla

Beat all together and put on top of pudding. Decorate with cherries.

Apple Crisp Dessert

1 cup flour
½ cup butter
½ teaspoon cinnamon

2 tablespoons sugar
1½ cups brown sugar
6 apples

Slice apples and put in pan that has been greased. Mix and pour rest of ingredients over apples. Bake at 350° for 30 minutes.

Fruit Whip Dessert

12 oz. frozen whipped topping
1 small can crushed pineapple drained
1 cup pecans

8 oz. cherries
7 oz. condensed milk

Mix together and refrigerate for 2 hours.

Frosted Pecans Dessert

1 pound pecans
½ cup water
1 tablespoon corn syrup
1 teaspoon butter rum syrup
1 tablespoon corn syrup

1 cup sugar
2 tablespoons butter
1 teaspoon vanilla
1 teaspoon almond syrup

Measure the vanilla, almond syrup and butter rum syrup in a cup. Add these 3 just before you add the pecans. Heat pecans in oven just till warm. Boil sugar, water, butter and corn syrup together, till it threads off spoon, stirring constantly, about 3 minutes. Now add all together and stir till nuts are coated. Drop in piles on a greased piece of foil. Cool.

Flo's Pistachio Pudding

1 sm. box instant pistachio pudding
1 sm. can crushed pineapple
12-oz. frozen whipped topping

1 cup miniature marshmallows
1 cup pecans
Cherries to decorate

Mix all together except cherries. Put in refrigerator to firm.

Apple Strawberry Layers

1 tablespoon cornstarch   1 tablespoon water

Dissolve the cornstarch in the water. Add the 2 following ingredients:

1 21-oz. can apple pie filling (chop the apples)
¼ cup sugar

Spray a 9 x 12-inch baking dish with nonstick spray. Spread the above in the dish.

Layer 2:
1 can of flaky biscuits (8 biscuits)

Cut each biscuit into 25 pieces or pull apart the flaky layers, and completely cover the apple filling.

Layer 3:
1 tablespoon cornstarch   1 tablespoon water

Dissolve the cornstarch in the water; add the 2 following ingredients:

1 21-oz. can strawberry pie filling   ¼ cup sugar

Spread on top of the biscuits.

Layer 4:
1½ cups brown sugar   1 cup flour
1 cup frosted flakes cereal   1 cup pecans (chopped)
1 stick melted butter   1 teaspoon vanilla
1 teaspoon danish pastry extract

Mix completely. Spread on top of the strawberry pie filling. Bake at 375° for 30 minutes.

Karen's Gelatin and Cheese Dessert

1 3-oz. box gelatin any flavor   1 cup water
¾ cup sugar   1 cup whipping cream
1 cup Cheddar cheese grated   1 cup pecans
1 small can crushed pineapple with juice
1½ cups miniature marshmallows

Dissolve gelatin in water. Boil sugar and pineapple till sugar is melted. Mix into gelatin. Cool till almost set. Whip. Add grated cheese. Fold cream, pecans and marshmallows into gelatin. Refrigerate till set.

Pudding Roll Dessert

1 3-oz. box instant vanilla pudding
1 1.3-oz. pkg. dry whipped topping
1 jelly roll

1½ cups milk
1 cup whipping cream

Beat the first 4 above ingredients together. Spread jelly on the jelly roll and slice ½-inch thick. Arrange slices around the side of a clear deep dish. Pour pudding on top, and refrigerate.

Vanilla Rice Pudding Dessert

3 cups milk (divided)
1 pkg. dry whipped topping
1 pkg. vanilla instant pudding (4 serving size)

1 cup instant rice
2 teaspoons vanilla

Boil 1 cup of the milk, stir in the rice and cover. Let stand 5 minutes. Prepare the instant pudding with the other 2 cups of milk, vanilla and dry whipped topping. Beat till thick. Mix the rice and pudding; cover with plastic wrap. Let cool 10 minutes.

Country Strawberry Pretzel Dessert

2 cups crushed pretzels
1 cup plus 2 tablespoons sugar

¾ cup melted butter
1 cup pecans

Mix the 4 above ingredients. Press into a 9 x 12-inch greased pan. Bake at 400° for 4 minutes. Cool completely.

8 oz. cream cheese
8-oz. whipped topping (frozen kind)

½ cup sugar
2 teaspoons vanilla

Beat the 4 above ingredients together; spread on crust.

2 cups boiling water
2 10-oz. frozen strawberries
1 8-oz. crushed pineapple (drain and save ½ cup of juice)

1 6-oz. strawberry gelatin
½ cup pineapple juice

Dissolve gelatin in boiling water, add pineapple and strawberries. Chill till thick. Pour over cream cheese. Refrigerate.

Strawberry Cobbler

2 cans (21-oz.) strawberry pie filling
3 oz. cream cheese
1 box yellow cake mix

½ cup butter
2 teaspoons vanilla

Pour pie filling into a greased 13 x 9 x 2-inch baking dish. Bake at 350° for 5 or 7 minutes till heated through. In mixing bowl cream butter, cream cheese and vanilla. Place cake mix in another bowl. Cut in cream cheese mixture till crumbly. Sprinkle over hot filling. Bake 25 or 30 minutes until topping is golden brown. Serves 12.

Fruit Cobbler

1¾ cups of the 3 following ingredients combined: 1 envelope dry whipped topping,
    1 small box vanilla cook pudding, rest flour
1½ cups sugar
2 teaspoons baking powder
1 teaspoon vanilla
1 qt. can drained peaches
½ cup coconut

1½ cups milk
2 large eggs
1 can of fruit cocktail (drained)
6 cherries (cut up)
1 cup pecans

Mix fruit and pecans into batter. Put in deep oblong cake pan lined with foil. Bake at 350° for 30 minutes uncovered and 45 minutes covered with foil. If using fresh peaches, add ¾ cup more sugar.

Evelyn's Quickie Cobbler

1½ cups flour
1½ cups milk
1 teaspoon vanilla
1 cup pecans
Cherries for color

1½ cups sugar
2 egg whites
2 teaspoons baking powder
½ cup coconut

Melt 2 tablespoons margarine in 8 x 13-inch baking dish. Layer bottom of dish with drained fruit cocktail or peaches. Pour the above over the fruit. Bake at 350° for 50 minutes.

1950 Granny's Peach Cobbler

1 stick butter melted
¾ cup flour
1 teaspoon baking powder
2½ cups drained peaches or pears

½ cup sugar
¾ cup milk
1 teaspoon vanilla
½ teaspoon cinnamon

Mix all together and bake at 450° for 20 minutes.

Seasonal Peach Cobbler

1 cup flour
1¼ cups sugar
¾ cup milk
1 29-oz. can peaches

½ cup butter
2 teaspoons baking powder
1 teaspoon vanilla

Melt butter in 8 x 10-inch baking dish. Mix sugar, flour and baking powder; add milk. Pour mixture on top of melted butter but do not mix. Add peaches, juice and all. Preheat oven to 375° and bake for 40 minutes.

Evelyn's Fresh Peach Cobbler

¾ cup flour
1 stick butter (melted)
¾ cup sugar
½ teaspoon cinnamon
½ teaspoon butter flavoring
2½ cups fresh peaches preferred or canned peaches drained

2 eggs
¾ cup milk
2 teaspoons baking powder
1 teaspoon vanilla

Beat all ingredients except peaches together with a mixer. Stir in peaches. Pour into a 9-inch pie plate, sprayed with nonstick spray. Bake at 400° for 45 minutes or till done. Cover last 20 minutes.

Peachy Fruit Cobbler

½ cup butter
1½ cups sugar
½ cup condensed milk
1 teaspoon cinnamon
½ cup fruit cocktail juice
1 teaspoon vanilla

1 cup flour + 1 tablespoon
3 teaspoons baking powder
1 can fruit cocktail drained
3 cups fresh peaches or canned
1 cup pecans

Beat the butter, sugar, condensed milk, fruit juice and the flavorings till well mixed. Add flour, cinnamon and baking powder, beat till thoroughly mixed. Stir in fruit and pecans. Pour into a 9 x 12-inch Pyrex baking dish that has been sprayed with nonstick spray. Bake at 350° for 1 hour.

Grandmo's Pear Cobbler

2 quarts peeled, diced pears (about 12 large pears)
1 stick margarine
2 cups self-rising flour
1 cup milk
2 teaspoons vanilla

2 cups sugar divided
1 stick margarine melted
½ teaspoon cinnamon

Place pears in large pot; add water to cover pears. Cook over medium high heat until pears are tender. Drain pears, reserve 1 cup liquid in pan.

Add: ½ cup margarine and 1 cup sugar to hot cooked pears.

Combine remaining 1 cup sugar and flour in a bowl.

Add ½ cup melted margarine and milk. Mix well, using a whisk, until mixture is smooth. Pour into a 13 x 9 x 2-inch baking dish, sprayed with nonstick spray. Top with pear mixture. Sprinkle cinnamon evenly over pears. Bake at 375° for 30 minutes.

Texas Peach Cobbler

½ cup butter
3 teaspoons baking powder
1 cup milk
3 cups fresh peaches or canned peaches drained

1 cup flour
2 cups sugar
1 teaspoon cinnamon

Preheat oven 350°. Melt butter in 8 x 12-inch baking dish. Sift flour. Mix together flour, 1 cup sugar, salt and baking powder. Blend with milk. Pour mixture over melted butter. Spread peaches over this and sprinkle with other cup of sugar mixed with cinnamon. Bake 1 hour. Crust will magically appear and cover entire surface of cobbler.

Fresh Apple Cobbler

1 tablespoon + 1 teaspoon cornstarch
5 cups sliced apples
¼ teaspoon salt
2 tablespoons butter

1 cup sugar
½ teaspoon cinnamon
2 teaspoons vanilla
4 tablespoons milk

Mix the above and turn into a 9-inch baking pan.

Batter:
2 large eggs
1 teaspoon baking powder
3 tablespoons butter

¾ cup sugar
½ cup flour
⅛ teaspoon salt

Beat well. Pour batter over the filling. Bake at 350° for about 40 minutes or until apples are tender.

Derek Krause—Champion of Cobblers

Preheat oven to 350°

1 white cake mix
1 quart peaches or cherries or fruit cocktail
2 eggs

1 can 7-Up

Beat on high speed the eggs, cake mix and 7-Up until smooth. Pour ½ of the batter in a greased cobbler pan. Put the drained fruit on top of the batter, then put the last half of batter on top of fruit. Bake till golden brown.

Grandpa's Peach Cobbler

3½ cups sliced peaches
½ cup plus 1 tablespoon flour
¼ cup sugar
2 teaspoons vanilla

1 stick butter
1 cup brown sugar
1 teaspoon cinnamon

Preheat oven to 350°. Sprinkle ½ cup brown sugar over peaches. Pour into a deep buttered pie plate. In separate bowl put butter, flour, sugars, vanilla and cinnamon. Blend into course pieces and sprinkle over peaches. Bake about 30 minutes.

Southern Apple Cobbler

1 18½-oz. box white cake mix
1 cup pecans
½ teaspoon cinnamon

1 cup butter
½ cup milk
2 21-oz. cans apple pie filling

Preheat oven to 375°

Step 1: Place the apple filling in a 13 x 9-inch greased dish.
Step 2: In a mixing bowl put the cake mix and butter; mix till crumbly.
Step 3: Remove 1½ cups batter; stir in pecans and cinnamon; mix well.
Step 4: Add the milk to step 2, beat the milk in till all is moistened.
Step 5: Spread step 4 over the apple filling.
Step 6. Spread step 3 over all.

Bake for 35 to 45 minutes or till golden brown.

Rich Cream Ice Cream

6 eggs beaten and strained   1½ cups sugar

Add enough milk just to cook the eggs and sugar just to a boil.
Add:

1 can condensed milk
1 small box vanilla instant pudding
1 tablespoon vanilla

1 large can evaporated milk
1 pint whipping cream

Add enough milk to make 3½ quarts (for 1 gallon ice cream freezer).

Limited Richness Ice Cream

6 eggs beaten and strained   2 cups sugar

Add enough milk to cook the eggs and sugar, just to a boil. Add:

1 can condensed milk
1 small box vanilla instant pudding

1 large can evaporated milk
1 tablespoon vanilla

Add enough milk to make 3½ quarts (for 1 gallon ice cream freezer).

Delicious Ice Cream

2¼ cups sugar   8 eggs beaten

Cook eggs and sugar with about 4 cups milk, to a boil, and cool.
Add:

1 small box vanilla instant pudding   1 tablespoon vanilla
1½ cups evaporated milk (1 large can)   2 cups half and half
2 cans condensed milk   1 teaspoon salt

Stir in enough milk to fill ice cream freezer. Mix and pour into a 6-quart ice cream freezer.

Country Peach or Apple Pie

2 tablespoons butter or margarine
2 cups sliced apples or canned or fresh peaches
1 large can refrigerated flaky biscuits
1 cup chopped pecans   ½ cup brown sugar
¼ teaspoon cinnamon   ½ cup corn syrup
1½ teaspoons whiskey   2 large eggs
½ teaspoon Danish pastry extract   2 tablespoons cornstarch

Grease a 8 x 12-inch baking dish. Spread ½ the fruit; cut the unbaked biscuits in very small pieces and place on fruit. Put the other ½ of the fruit on top of the biscuits; sprinkle the pecans on top.

Beat well the following: brown sugar, cinnamon, corn syrup, whiskey, eggs, cornstarch and Danish pastry extract. When well beaten, pour over the fruit, biscuits and pecans.

Bake at 350° for 1 hour or till golden brown. Remove from oven and let stand for 5 minutes. Pour the glaze over.

Glaze:
½ cup powdered sugar   ½ teaspoon vanilla
½ teaspoon Danish Pastry Extract

Blend with enough milk for desired drizzling consistency. Drizzle over warm cake. Serve warm or cold. Store in refrigerator.

Summertime Strawberry Cream Cheese Pie

1 9-inch baked pie crust

1 can condensed milk   1 8-oz. cream cheese

2 teaspoons vanilla   3½ cups fresh strawberries

1 (16-oz.) jar strawberry glaze

Beat cheese till fluffy. Add the condensed milk and vanilla. Beat till smooth. Pour into pie crust. Chill 4 hours. Put strawberries on top of filling. Pour glaze over. Keep refrigerated.

Two Way Velvety Custard Pie

1 9-inch unbaked pie shell

4 large eggs   ¾ cup sugar

¼ teaspoon salt   2 teaspoons vanilla

2½ cups scalded milk   Sprinkle nutmeg on top

Beat eggs, sugar, salt and vanilla. Slowly, stir in hot milk. At once, pour into unbaked pie shell. Bake at 475° for 5 minutes. Reduce heat to 425° for 10 minutes. Insert knife in center; if comes out clean, remove and cool.

Idea: Omit nutmeg, mix 1 small box strawberry gelatin according to directions on box. Let set till still pourable. Pour on top of pie. Top gelatin with whipped topping. Strawberries for decoration.

The Country Apple Cream Pie

4 cups sliced apples   4 tablespoons sugar

Sprinkle of lemon juice to preserve color of apples.

¼ cup butter   8 oz. cream cheese

1 pkg. 3.4 oz. instant vanilla pudding   1½ cups milk

1 baked 9-inch pie shell

¼ cup apricot or strawberry preserves

In large skillet sauté apples, sugar and lemon juice and butter until apples are tender cool. In mixing bowl, beat the cream cheese till smooth. Gradually beat in milk, dry pudding mix and lemon juice. Beat until thickened. Spread into pastry shell; arrange apples over filling. Brush with preserves. Refrigerate for 1 hour before serving.

Country Boston Cream Pie

3 eggs separated
1½ cups flour
2 tablespoons milk

1 cup sugar
1 teaspoon baking powder
2 teaspoons vanilla

Beat egg yolks until light. Gradually add sugar, mix well. Slowly add milk, then flour mixture. Add vanilla; beat egg whites till soft peaks. Fold into batter. Line 2 (9-inch) cake pans with wax paper. Divide batter. Bake at 375° for 20 minutes or until inserted wooden pick comes clean; cool thoroughly.

Split each layer into 2. Spread layers with vanilla instant pudding and chocolate pudding. Make sure vanilla pudding is on top, then mix cocoa syrup with maple syrup to drizzle on top of vanilla pudding.

Glaze:
¼ cup chocolate syrup

1 teaspoon maple syrup

Creative Meringue

Mix:
1 tablespoon sugar
½ cup water

1½ tablespoons cornstarch

Cook till thick. Cover with plastic wrap. No hard film on top. Cool.

3 egg whites
1 teaspoon vanilla

4 tablespoons sugar

Beat eggs, sugar and vanilla till stiff. Add the cool cornstarch mixture, small amounts at a time. Beat with electric mixer on high for about 2 minutes. Spread on pie and bake at 350° till golden brown.

No Fail Meringue

3 egg whites

1 cup marshmallow creme

Beat egg whites and a dash of salt until soft peaks form. Gradually add marshmallow creme, beating until stiff peaks form. Spread over pie, sealing to edge of crust. Bake at 350° till golden brown.

Fool Proof Meringue

Mix 1 tablespoon cornstarch and 2 tablespoons sugar with ½ cup water; cook together until clear, then cover.

Add a dash of salt to 4 egg whites and whip until standing peaks, at which time you add the above mixture. Continue beating until creamy, then add 4 tablespoons sugar gradually, beating until very creamy.

Pile on pie and bake about 30 minutes at 325° or until golden brown.

Pecan Nut Crust

1½ cups pecans chopped   3 egg whites
4 tablespoons sugar

Mix pecans and sugar. Beat egg whites. Fold into pecans and sugar. Spread into pie plate, and fill with your favorite filling.

Wafer Pudding Pie

48 vanilla wafer cookies

Place 25 wafers on bottom of a greased 9-inch pie plate.

2 small boxes instant vanilla pudding
4 oz. frozen topping   1 can condensed milk
3 cups milk   2 teaspoons vanilla

Beat the 5 above ingredients till thick.

4 bananas sliced, dipped in lemon juice to prevent discoloring.

Put a layer of pudding on the wafers, and a layer of bananas, and wafers. Continue layering till used up. Then cover top with 4 oz. frozen topping, and refrigerate.

Extra Easy Apple Pie

1 cup pancake or waffle mix
½ cup brown sugar
3 cups sliced apples
¼ teaspoon nutmeg
½ cup milk

¾ cup pecans
3 tablespoons butter
1 teaspoon cinnamon
¾ cup sugar
3 eggs

In a bowl combine ½ cup pancake mix, pecans and brown sugar. Cut in 2 tablespoons butter until mixture resembles coarse crumbs; set aside.

In a bowl combine apples, cinnamon and nutmeg. Spread into a greased 9-inch pie plate. Combine sugar, milk, eggs, remaining pancake mix and butter. Stir until smooth. Pour over apples. Sprinkle with crumb mixture. Bake at 325° for 40 to 45 minutes or until knife inserted in center comes clean.

Mock Apple Pie

1½ cups sugar
2 teaspoons cream of tartar

2 cups water
21 Ritz crackers

Boil 2 minutes. Add: 21 Ritz crackers. Boil 2 more minutes. Pour into an uncooked 9-inch pie crust dotted with butter. Sprinkle cinnamon. Cover with top crust. Sprinkle with sugar and cinnamon. Bake at 375° until golden brown.

Evelyn's Apple Pecan Pie
(No Crust)

¾ cup flour
1½ teaspoons baking powder
1 teaspoon vanilla
1 cup pecans

¾ cup sugar
1 large egg beaten
1 cup chopped apples

Bake in greased 9-inch pie pan. Bake at 300° for 1 hour.

Flaky Pie Crust

4½ cups flour
3 sticks butter

3 teaspoons sugar

Mix the above.
Add:

½ cup ice water

2 teaspoons red wine vinegar

Roll out. Makes 2 pie crusts.

Apple Skillet Pie

¾ cup vegetable oil
½ teaspoon baking powder
1 teaspoon cinnamon
2 apples or 1 can pears drained
¾ cup pecans

1½ cups flour
½ teaspoon salt
1 cup sugar
1 egg

Mix all the above. Put in cast iron skillet. Bake at 350° for 30 to 40 minutes.

Evelyn's Best Pecan Pie

1 cup white corn syrup or maple syrup
1 tablespoon corn syrup
2 tablespoons butter
1½ cup pecans

3 eggs
1 cup sugar
1½ teaspoons vanilla
1 9-inch unbaked pie crust

Combine all ingredients except pecans and put in blender. Stir in pecans. Pour into pie crust. Bake at 350°. Cover pie with foil after 30 minutes of baking. Bake 35 minutes more (about 65 minutes or till set).

Eleanor V. No Roll Pie Crust 1980

1½ cups flour
1 teaspoon salt
2 tablespoons cold water

1½ teaspoons sugar
½ cup oil

Press out in pie plate. Bake at 425° for about 12 minutes.

Buttermilk Pecan Pie

½ cup butter
6 eggs
2 teaspoons vanilla
1½ cups pecans

2 cups sugar
3 tablespoons flour
1 cup buttermilk
2 9-inch pie crusts unbaked

Combine all ingredients except pecans, beating well. Stir in pecans. Pour into the pie crusts. Bake at 325° for 1 hour or until done or when inserted knife comes clean. Last 30 minutes cover with foil.

Lillian's Heavenly Pecan Pie

3 egg whites
1 teaspoon baking powder
2 teaspoons vanilla

1 cup sugar
1 cup crushed graham crackers
1 cup pecans

Beat all together, except stir in pecans. Pour into greased pie pan. Bake at 350° for 30 minutes or till knife inserted comes clean.

Coconut Marshmallow Pie 50's

2 cups sugar
16 marshmallows
1 cup coconut

¾ cup water
4 egg whites stiffly beaten
1 cup pecans

Cook sugar and water till thick. Put in marshmallows and melt. Beat slowly into the stiffly beaten egg whites. Add pecans and coconut. Pour into a baked pie shell. Bake at 350° till lightly brown.

Chocolate Snow Pie

4 oz. square sweet chocolate or ¼ cup baking cocoa
⅓ cup milk
3 oz. cream cheese (softened)
1 cup pecans

2 tablespoons sugar
8 oz. frozen whipped topping
1 graham cracker pie crust

Heat chocolate and 2 tablespoons milk over low heat, stirring until melted. Beat sugar into cream cheese; add remaining milk to chocolate. Beat smooth. Fold frozen whipped topping in. Blend until smooth; add pecans. Spoon mixture into crust. Freeze about 4 hours and serve.

No Crust Chocolate Pie

¼ cup baking cocoa
1 teaspoon vanilla
3 eggs beaten
3 tablespoons flour
1 cup chopped pecans

½ cup butter
1 teaspoon vanilla nut
1 cup sugar
¼ teaspoon salt

Melt butter over low heat with the cocoa. Remove from heat; add vanilla. In mixing bowl combine eggs, sugar, flour and salt. Beat with mixer just till blended. Do not overbeat; fold in cocoa mixture. Fold in pecans. Pour into a greased 9-inch pie plate. Bake at 350° for 1 hour or till knife inserted in center comes clean. Refrigerate overnight. Garnish with whipped cream or frozen whipped topping.

Delicious Banana Pie 1945

1 9-inch pie crust baked
1½ cups milk (1 small can evaporated milk and milk to make 1½ cups)

5 tablespoons flour   ¾ cup brown sugar
3 egg yolks   ½ cup butter
2 large bananas (mashed)   1 cup toasted coconut
1 teaspoon maple extract

Cook the above till thickened; pour into a baked pie shell.

Meringue:
3 egg whites   2 tablespoons sugar
½ teaspoon cream of tartar

Beat till stiff peaks form. Spread on pie, sealing all edges. Bake at 350° till meringue is lightly browned.

Mama's Perpaid Ice Cream Pie 1940

1 baked 9-inch pie crust

1¼ cups hot water, pour over 1 small box strawberry gelatin (or any flavor). Mix good and let stand in icebox for 20 minutes.

Add 1 pint ice cream (vanilla or whatever you want) to gelatin. Beat very well, put in baked pie shell and stand in icebox.

White Chocolate Strawberry Pie

1 9-inch graham cracker crust   6 oz. white baking chocolate squares
2 tablespoons milk   3 oz. cream cheese
⅔ cup powdered sugar   1 cup whipping cream (whipped)
2 cups sliced fresh strawberries 2 teaspoons vanilla

Melt the chocolate with the milk. Cool to room temperature. Beat the cream cheese and sugar till smooth. Beat in vanilla and chocolate (save some chocolate to drizzle over the strawberries). Fold in the whipped cream. Spread into crust; arrange strawberries on top. Drizzle saved chocolate over strawberries. Refrigerate for at least 1 hour. Store in refrigerator.

Coconut Cream Pie 50's

9-inch baked pie crust or graham cracker pie crust
½ cup flour or ¼ cup cornstarch   1 cup sugar
½ teaspoon salt   2½ cups milk
¾ cup coconut   1 teaspoon vanilla
3 egg yolks   3 egg whites well beaten

Cook in double boiler the milk, ¾ cup sugar, flour and salt until mixture thickens. Beat in egg yolks quickly 1 at a time. Continue cooking and stirring for 2 minutes. Stir in ½ cup coconut and vanilla; pour into pie crust. Fold remaining sugar into the beaten egg whites; continue beating until very stiff. Place on top of filling, close to edge of crust. Sprinkle remaining coconut on top. Bake at 425° for about 4 minutes.

Apple Pudding Pie

1 small box vanilla cook pudding   2 cups milk
½ cup sugar   ¼ cup cornstarch
1 teaspoon imitation butter flavoring   ½ teaspoon cinnamon
3 apples sliced (sprinkle lemon juice over apples to keep color)

Slice apples in pie crust. Combine other 6 ingredients. Mix and pour over apples. Bake at 375° for 45 to 55 minutes or till done.

Quick Strawberry Pie

1 baked 9-inch pie crust or 1 9-inch graham cracker crust
1 can condensed milk   4 egg yolks
4 teaspoons vanilla

Blend yolks, milk and vanilla till smooth. Pour into the pie crust (if using a flour crust cover the edges with foil). Bake at 350° for 9 minutes. Cool. Top with 1 can strawberry pie filling.

Frozen Apple Pie

2 pre-made pie crusts
1 cup sugar
⅛ teaspoon salt
½ teaspoon apple bake
1½ tablespoons cornstarch

4 tablespoons butter
1 teaspoon cinnamon
⅛ teaspoon nutmeg
6 peeled and sliced apples
¼ cup whiskey

Put sugar in pan over medium heat. Bring to boil and cook till caramelized. Add the butter, spices and apples. Cook 5 minutes or till apples are tender. Remove from heat, add whiskey and flambé the mixture. Cook another 1 to 3 minutes. Drain the mixture in a colander. (Save the juice for the sauce; freeze and use when you bake the pie.) Toss the apples with the cornstarch and spread out on a sheet pan to cool. Then put in a pie plate lined with the crust and cover with the second crust and seal edges. Cut V in center of pie. Wrap the pie with plastic and freeze.

To bake just remove from freezer, no need to thaw. Preheat oven to 425° and bake 10 minutes. Reduce heat to 375° and bake for about 1 hour or till golden brown.

Peach & Fruit Cocktail Pie

½ cup sugar
1 can condensed milk
1 tablespoon cornstarch
¼ cup butter

2 eggs
¼ cup brown sugar
½ teaspoon cinnamon
2 teaspoons vanilla

4 cups of peaches and fruit cocktail together (both drained very well)
1 (9-inch) unbaked pie shell

Beat all ingredients together till very smooth, except fruit. Then stir in fruit. Pour into pie shell. Bake at 350° for 40 to 60 minutes.

ET—Possible Pie

4 eggs
½ cup sugar
½ cup coconut
1 teaspoon vanilla

1 tablespoon butter
½ cup biscuit and pancake mix
1 cup milk

Put all ingredients in blender, blend 15 seconds. Bake at 350° in well-greased 9-inch pie plate for 40 minutes.

Mama's Lemon Meringue Pie

1 baked 9-inch pie crust
5 tablespoons cornstarch
½ cup lemon juice
2 cups water
3 tablespoons stick margarine

1½ cups sugar
4 egg yolks
2 teaspoons lemon peel grated
Dash of salt

Mix sugar, cornstarch and salt in saucepan; beat in yolks till smooth, then beat in water. Cook and stir constantly until thick and translucent. Remove from heat. Beat in lemon juice, peel and margarine. Beat till smooth and pour into pie crust; top with meringue. Preheat oven to 350°.

Meringue:
4 egg whites
5 tablespoons sugar

½ teaspoon cream of tartar
2 teaspoons vanilla

Beat till stiff, pile on pie. Bake till golden brown.

Country Peaches and Cream Pie

¾ cup flour
½ teaspoon salt
¼ teaspoon nutmeg
1 egg
¼ cup vanilla or coconut dessert mix

1½ teaspoons baking powder
½ cup sugar
3 tablespoons butter
½ cup milk

2 cans peaches (14½ - 16 oz. each) sliced and drained (reserve juice)
8 oz. cream cheese
1½ teaspoons vanilla
¼ cup vanilla or coconut dessert mix

½ cup sugar
1 teaspoon vanilla nut
3 tablespoons peach juice

1 tablespoon sugar

½ teaspoon cinnamon

Spray bottom of a 10-inch pie plate. In large mixing bowl, combine the first 9 ingredients. Beat with mixer on medium speed for 2 minutes; pour into prepared pie plate. Set aside 8 large peach slices to decorate top of pie. Put the remaining peach slices over batter, keeping peaches about ½ to 1 inch from edge of pie plate.

In mixing bowl combine rest of ingredients except cinnamon and sugar. Beat till smooth and spoon over peaches with same distance from edge. Combine sugar and cinnamon; sprinkle over cream cheese filling. Place the 8 slices on top in circular fan design. Bake at 350° for 40 to 50 minutes. Chill till serving time.

Ann's Chocolate Pie

4 oz. bar chocolate   ½ cup butter
2 teaspoons vanilla

Melt butter and chocolate over low heat. Add vanilla and cool. Beat the following for 3 minutes at high speed:

3 eggs   1 cup sugar
3 tablespoons flour   ¼ teaspoon baking powder

Add chocolate mixture plus:

1 cup pecans   ½ cup coconut

Bake in 9- or 10-inch pie dish which has been lightly greased with margarine. Bake at 325° for 45 minutes.

Delicious Apple or Peach Pie

9-inch unbaked pie crust (flour kind)
Apples peeled and sliced (fill crust to heaping) or
Peaches frozen or fresh thawed and drained (fill crust to heaping)

Mix:
¾ cup sugar   ½ teaspoon cinnamon
1 teaspoon lemon juice to protect fruit from discoloring

Sprinkle the above over filling. Mix the following till crumbly:

½ cup sugar   ¾ cup flour
⅓ cup butter   ½ teaspoon nutmeg
1½ tablespoons cornstarch

Sprinkle crumbly mixture on top of filling. Bake at 400° for about 1 hour or till done. Cover with foil last 15 minutes.

The Brownie Pie

3 egg whites   1 cup chopped pecans
Dash salt   1 teaspoon vanilla
¾ cup fine chocolate wafer crumbs   ¾ cup sugar

Beat egg whites and salt till soft peaks. Gradually add sugar, beating till stiff peaks form. Add rest of ingredients. Pour into a greased 9-inch pie plate. Bake at 325° for about 38 minutes. Cool. Top with sweetened beaten whipped cream.

Country Banana Coconut Cream Pie

1 baked 9-inch pie crust
1⅓ cups milk
1 can condensed milk
3 tablespoons butter
¾ cup coconut toasted

3 tablespoons cornstarch
½ cup sugar
4 egg yolks beaten
2 teaspoons vanilla
3 bananas

Dissolve cornstarch in water. Stir in condensed milk and beaten egg yolks. Cook and stir till thickened. Remove from heat; add butter and vanilla. Cool. Stir in coconut. Slice bananas dipped in lemon juice to prevent discoloration, arrange on pie crust. Pour filling over bananas.

Meringue: Beat the 4 egg whites with ¼ cup of sugar and ½ teaspoon cream of tartar till stiff peaks form; spread over pie. Bake at 350° till meringue is golden brown.

Streusel Apple Custard Pie

1 unbaked 9-inch pie crust
1 can (14-oz.) condensed milk
¼ cup butter
2 teaspoons cornstarch
Dash of nutmeg
4 tablespoons brown sugar

4 cups apples (sliced)
2 eggs
2 teaspoons vanilla
½ teaspoon cinnamon
½ cup pecans

Preheat oven to 425°. Spread sliced apples in pastry. Beat eggs. Beat in condensed milk, butter, cinnamon, nutmeg, vanilla and cornstarch. Pour over apples. Combine pecans and brown sugar. Sprinkle over pie. Bake 10 minutes. Reduce temperature to 350° and bake 35 or 40 minutes longer or till golden brown.

Any Flavor Ice Cream Pie

Dissolve 1 3-oz. box gelatin strawberry or any flavor in ½ cup boiling water. Stir in 3 cups of peaches (drained; thaw if frozen). Add 1 pint of ice cream vanilla or any flavor. Pour into 2 (8-inch) graham pie crusts. Put in refrigerator to set. Top with whipped cream or frozen whipped topping.

Ranch Pecan Chocolate Pie

Unbaked 9-inch pie crust
2 tablespoons flour
3 tablespoons baking cocoa
2 tablespoons white corn syrup
¾ cup evaporated milk undiluted

1½ cups sugar
½ cup butter
3 eggs
2 teaspoons vanilla
1 cup pecans

Put all except pecans in blender and blend till mixed. Stir in 1 cup pecans. Pour into crust and bake at 375° for 55 minutes. Cover with foil after 15 minutes of baking.

Best Chocolate Nut Pie

1 cup sugar
¼ teaspoon salt
2 tablespoons butter
1 tablespoon white corn syrup
1½ cups pecans
⅓ cup plus 1 heaping tablespoon flour

3 tablespoons baking cocoa
3 egg yolks
2 teaspoons vanilla
2 cups milk

Put all the above ingredients into a blender, except pecans, and blend for about 2 minutes. Pour into a pot. Cook, stirring constantly, till thick. When it gets thick, cook an extra minute. Remove from stove; stir in pecans. Then cover with wax paper directly on top to cool. Pour into baked 9-inch pastry shell.

Meringue: Beat 3 egg whites with ¼ teaspoon cream of tartar and 1 teaspoon vanilla till soft peaks form. Gradually add 6 teaspoons sugar; beat till stiff peaks form. Spread on top of pie. Bake in moderate oven 350° till golden brown about 15 minutes. When cooled, refrigerate for 2 hours minimum.

Evelyn's Chocolate Cream Pie

Baked 9-inch pie crust
1 cup sugar
¼ teaspoon salt
3 egg yolks
1 teaspoon vanilla

3 tablespoons baking cocoa
⅓ cup flour
2 cups milk
2 tablespoons butter
1 teaspoon vanilla nut extract

Blend ingredients in blender. Put in pot, stirring constantly, and cook till thick; cool. Pour in cool pie crust. Top with meringue.

Meringue: Beat 3 egg whites with ¼ teaspoon cream of tartar and 1 teaspoon vanilla till soft peaks form. Gradually add 2 tablespoons sugar. Beat till stiff peaks form; spread on top of pie. Bake at 350° for 15 minutes. Cool.

Sour Cream Peach Pie

Crust:
1½ cups flour   1 stick butter
½ teaspoon salt

Mix the above then press into a 9-inch pie plate.

Filling:
1¼ cups sugar   4 cups sliced fresh peaches
1 egg   2 tablespoons flour
¼ teaspoon salt   1 cup sour cream
2 teaspoons vanilla

Mix all ingredients, except fold in peaches. Pour into pie crust. Bake at 400° for 17 minutes. Then turn oven to 350° and bake for 22 minutes.

Topping:
½ cup flour   ½ stick margarine
½ teaspoon cinnamon

Mix till crumbly and sprinkle on top of pie. Bake at 400° for 9 minutes.

Grandmo's Egg Nog Pie

2 teaspoons non-flavored gelatin   2 tablespoons water

Soak the above together till dissolved.

¾ cup sugar   2 tablespoons + 1 teaspoon cornstarch

Mix these 2 ingredients.

1 cup milk scalded

Add milk to the sugar/cornstarch mixture and cook till thick.

4 egg yolks beaten

Add eggs to the milk mixture and cook 1 minute.

2 tablespoons butter   2 teaspoons vanilla

Add the butter and vanilla and gelatin mixture to the milk mixture; cool.

1½ cups whipped cream

Fold into the mixture and pour into a baked pie shell.

Black Beauty Chocolate Pie

3 tablespoons baking cocoa
2 cups milk
3 tablespoons cornstarch
1 tablespoon butter
1 teaspoon vanilla nut
2 tablespoons white corn syrup

1½ cups sugar
3 egg yolks
¼ teaspoon salt
1 teaspoon vanilla

Put all ingredients in blender, then cook till thick. Cool. Pour into a baked 9-inch pie crust.

Meringue:
3 egg whites
1 teaspoon vanilla
½ teaspoon cream of tartar

4 tablespoons sugar
¼ teaspoon baking powder

Beat till stiff peaks form. Put on pie. Bake at 350° till golden brown.

Glaze for Pie Crust

Mix egg white and milk, brush on pie crust for a beautiful glaze.

Evelyn's Strawberry Delight Pie

3 cups fresh strawberries—sliced   ¼ cup sugar

Mix the sugar and strawberries together; set aside.

3 eggs beaten   ½ cup sugar
2 tablespoons butter

Beat the 3 above ingredients together, then add:

1 teaspoon vanilla   ¾ cup biscuit and pancake mix
1 teaspoon baking powder

Beat all ingredients together, except strawberries. Pour into a greased 9-inch pie plate. Pour fresh strawberry mixture over top. Bake at 375° for 25 minutes. Put frozen whipped topping and sliced fresh strawberries on top.

Note: *Bake ready made pie crust at 450° for 15 minutes.*

Honey Pecan Pie

½ cup honey
¼ cup butter
1 cup pecans

½ cup brown sugar
3 eggs beaten
1 9-inch unbaked pie crust

Blend honey and sugar together. Cook slowly to form syrup. Add butter. Add beaten eggs and pecans. Pour in pie crust. Bake at 400° for 10 minutes. Reduce temp. to 350° and bake 30 minutes or until knife comes clean.

Best Custard Apple Pie

¼ cup sugar
1 stick butter

1½ cups flour

Mix till crumbly; press into 9-inch pie plate. Arrange 3 cups sliced apples over crust. Mix and sprinkle ½ cup sugar and ½ teaspoon cinnamon over apples. Bake at 375° for 20 minutes.

Custard:
1 cup evaporated milk
½ cup sugar

2 eggs

Blend together and pour over apples. Bake at 375° for 25 to 30 minutes or till knife inserted comes clean.

Puddin' Pie

1 9-inch graham cracker crust
1 cup powdered sugar

2 8-oz. cream cheese

Beat cream cheese and sugar till smooth; pour into pie crust. Sprinkle ¾ cup pecans on cream cheese mixture.

Mix the following and pour over the above:
1 small box instant chocolate pudding mix
1 small box instant vanilla pudding mix
2 cups milk

2 teaspoons vanilla

Refrigerate till set. Top with frozen whipped topping and pecans.

Main Dishes, Casseroles, Salads, Soups & Vegetables

Parsley Rice

Rice (2 cups instant rice or 1 cup long-grain dry rice)
2 cups water   Salt
¼ cup margarine   ½ cup fresh parsley

Simmer for 15 minutes or cook according to instant rice directions.

Evelyn's Mexican Rice

1 cup rice browned in 2 tablespoons of bacon grease

Put in 1 at a time:
½ teaspoon dry garlic   Pinch of salt
¼ teaspoon dry jalapeño   2 teaspoons dry tomatoes
2 teaspoons dry zucchini squash   1 teaspoon pinto bean seasoning
½ teaspoon chili powder   ½ teaspoon fajita seasoning

Add:
¼ cup diced bell pepper   ½ cup chopped onion

Sauté the above. Then add 3 cups water. Simmer till tender.

Cheesy Egg Noodles

1 cup egg noodles   1 tablespoon avocado oil
Salt to taste
Water (enough to cook noodles 7 minutes)

Drain noodles and add:

¼ cup butter or margarine   ¼ cup chopped onion
½ cup seasoned stuffing mix   1 teaspoon garlic oil
1 teaspoon olive oil   1 teaspoon dry parsley
½ cup Velveeta or cheese spread

Put in microwave to melt cheese.

Cheese Potatoes

In a baking dish put potatoes sliced ¼-inch thick; stir in onion. Salt and pepper and add margarine. Put in microwave, cook till tender. When done, grate some Cheddar cheese on top. Put back into microwave and melt cheese. About 25 minutes to cook.

Mashed Potato Pancakes

1 cup mashed potatoes
1 tablespoon baking powder
½ teaspoon salt

½ cup flour
1 beaten eggs
Pepper to taste

Combine the above; form into pancakes. Fry both sides till brown.

Fancy Black Eye Peas

Sauté the following:
1 tablespoon garlic oil
1 tablespoon olive oil
½ cup onion
¼ cup red bell pepper

1 tablespoon avocado oil
½ cup chopped bacon
½ cup bell pepper

In the bean pot put the following:
1 cup black eyes
Salt to taste

Water to cover
1 small jar pimientos

Add the sauté mixture and cook till tender. And at the last few minutes add: ½ cup instant rice. *Um-um-delicious!*

Simple Blackeyes

1 medium red bell pepper chopped
1 medium green bell pepper chopped
1 tablespoon bacon grease

1 medium onion chopped
½ cup ham chopped
1 clove garlic chopped

Sauté the above. Add the following:

salt and pepper to taste
dash of Italian salad dressing blend

dash of pizza seasoning
1 lb. dry black eye peas

Water about 2 inches above peas in pot. You will have to add more water. Cook peas till tender, about 1½ hours.

Instant Sweet Vanilla Rice

4 cups milk
1¼ cups sugar
1 cup instant rice

¼ cup margarine
1 teaspoon vanilla

Boil milk, sugar, vanilla and margarine. Add rice. Turn heat off and cover.

Feast Buttery Stuffing

1 lb. pork breakfast sausage (crumbled and fried)
4 cups day old bread (toast bread slices)
1 can chicken broth
1 cup butter (melted)

Pour broth and butter over bread slices to soak; mash up.

1 small jar mushrooms and juice
1 cup chopped onion
1 teaspoon poultry seasoning
1½ teaspoons thyme
¼ cup parsley

4 eggs
1 cup celery chopped
½ teaspoon sage
Salt and pepper to taste
1 small jar pimientos

Mix all ingredients together; put into a greased casserole dish. Bake at 350° for 30 minutes covered, 10 to 15 minutes uncovered, or until lightly toasted.

Great Egg Noodles & Sweet Peas

1 can mushroom soup
1 tablespoon vegetable flakes
½ cup mozzarella cheese

1 can water
1 tablespoon margarine
1½ cups egg noodles

Bring all except noodles to a boil slowly. Add egg noodles; cook slowly for 7 minutes. Turn off heat and cover. Let noodles soak till tender.

Best Spaghetti

3 cups water
1 teaspoon parsley
Salt to taste
1 tablespoon dry onion or 2 tablespoons fresh onion
1 teaspoon Italian Salad Blend Dressing

2 cups spaghetti
½ cup margarine

Cook till tender.

Veggie Rice Pilaf

¾ cup rice
1 can (14 oz.) chicken broth ¼ teaspoon basil
1 cup mixed frozen vegetables 1 tablespoon margarine
⅓ cup sweet bell peppers chopped 1 small onion chopped

Cook all together till done, about 15 minutes, in covered saucepan.

Weekly Grand White Beans

Cook 2 cups white beans to half cooked. Then add the following.

Fry:
6 slices bacon ¼ cup onions
4 cloves of garlic

Add the following:
Cayenne pepper Salt to taste
1 medium fresh tomato 1 bay leaf
1 teaspoon mustard 1 can beer
1 tablespoon brown sugar ½ jigger whiskey
1 tablespoon Worcestershire sauce

Add the white beans. Cook till tender.

Country Sauerkraut

Drain liquid from sauerkraut; rinse with clear water 2 times. Squeeze water from sauerkraut both times. Then cover sauerkraut with water. Add a dash of black pepper and 1 tablespoon bacon grease per quart of sauerkraut. Cook on medium heat, till all of water has been cooked out. About 40 minutes.

Baked Beans

1 cup pinto beans 1 cup white beans
4 slices fried bacon ½ medium onion
1 jalapeño 5 cloves garlic
1 tablespoon brown sugar ¼ cup corn syrup
1 small can tomato sauce 1 teaspoon mustard
1 can chicken broth Dash of salt and black pepper

Cover with water (will have to add water gradually). Put all together in baking dish and bake at 350° till tender.

Healthy Potato Dish

Sauté ½ lb. bacon till crisp and add ½ cup onion.

Now layer the rest in order given on top of the bacon and onions:

¼ cup diced red bell pepper
1 cup sliced potatoes
1 cup sliced carrots
¼ cup diced green bell pepper
½ cup green peas
½ cup macaroni
1 cup sliced yellow or zucchini squash
Sprinkle with salt, pepper and brisket rub
¾ cup shredded longhorn cheese on top

Cover pot and cook very slow till potatoes are tender.

Evelyn's Spaghetti Veggies (Nu-Nus)

1 fresh tomato peeled and chopped
1 clove of garlic chopped
½ medium bell pepper chopped
½ teaspoon Italian seasoning
½ teaspoon Creole and Cajun seasoning
½ medium onion chopped
1 stick celery chopped
½ cup margarine
½ teaspoon Nature's Seasons
½ teaspoon Krazy Salt

Put the above in pot and cover with water; boil about 10 minutes. May have to add more water. Add 2 cups spaghetti or 1 cup macaroni. Cook till done, about 8 minutes.

Potato Patties 50's

2 cups mashed potatoes
1 teaspoon baking powder
½ teaspoon salt
½ cup flour
1 egg
Pepper to taste

Combine the above ingredients. Form into pancake-size patties and fry on both sides till golden brown.

Evelyn's Supreme Spanish Rice

1 tablespoon grapeseed oil, garlic, and parsley
1 tablespoon grapeseed oil, citrus, and cilantro

½ cup margarine	1 stalk chopped celery
½ medium onion chopped	1 medium bell pepper chopped
1 slice lunch ham chopped	

Cook the above in a saucepan till tender. Add:

¾ cup tomato sauce	1¼ cups instant rice

Add a dash of the following:

garlic and spice	cumin
fajita seasoning	fiesta seasoning
cilantro	Italian salad dressing spice
salsa seasoning	seasoning salt
Nature's Seasons	

Add about 1 cup water, just enough to tenderize rice. Cook till tender, with slow heat, about 5 minutes.

Spinach Balls 60's

1 box frozen spinach (cooked)	1 medium onion
1 cup stuffing mix	1 stick butter
¼ cup parmesan cheese	Pinch garlic powder
Pinch thyme	1 egg
Pepper	

Mix and make into balls and place on greased cookie sheet. Place red tomato slice on top of each. Bake at 350° for 20 minutes.

Mustard	Chicken broth
Salt and black pepper	Water

Put together in baking dish; add balls and bake at 350° till tender.

Proud Lima Beans

1 cup lima beans	1 cup broccoli
½ cup cauliflower	½ cup carrots
1 teaspoon season-all	½ cup margarine
Salt to taste	1 teaspoon soup and vegetable seasoning

Water about 1½ inches over beans in pot.

Vegetable Rice

1 cup broccoli
¼ cup chopped onion
1½ cups water
1 teaspoon Krazy Salt
½ teaspoon soup and vegetable seasoning

½ cup yellow squash
¼ cup margarine
½ teaspoon thyme
½ teaspoon Nature's Seasons

Cook for 18 minutes. Add 1½ cups instant rice, turn burner off, let set till rice is tender.

Evelyn's Best Pinto Beans

My husband says these are the best beans he ever ate.

2 cups dry pinto beans washed

Put in pot and cover with water, bring to boil, turn burner off. Let beans soak 30 minutes. Drain, rinse with hot tap water. Put the beans and the following ingredients in a 6-qt. slow cooker:

Ham bone
1 tablespoon mustard
½ teaspoon cilantro
½ cup fresh green onions
1 teaspoon Creole and Cajun seasoning
1 fresh peeled tomato (no canned tomatoes)
1 bulb garlic (bulb not a clove of garlic)

1 tablespoon bacon grease
1 teaspoon dry jalapeño
½ teaspoon Italian seasoning
1 tablespoon Pinto Bean seasoning
Salt to taste

In slow cooker set on high for 5 hours.

Speckled Rice

1 cup regular rice
¼ cup margarine
1 teaspoon parsley flakes

1 cup water
1 tablespoon chopped onion
Salt

Cook 15 minutes at simmer, after boiling.

Delicious Sweet Instant Rice

4 cups milk
1 tablespoon margarine
1 cup instant rice

1 cup sugar
1 teaspoon vanilla

Boil milk, sugar, margarine and vanilla together. Add rice and simmer for 5 minutes. Pour in bowl; dot with margarine and sprinkle with cinnamon.

Delicious Country Dressing

1 oz. onion and garlic croutons
½ cup chopped onion
1 can chicken broth
¾ lb. pork breakfast sausage

16 oz. stuffing herb seasoned
1 cup chopped celery
1 small jar pimientos
1 can mushroom soup

Dash of the following:
Nature's Seasons
Garlic and Herb seasoning
1 oz. seasoned with 5 savory herbs stuffing mix

Creole and Cajun seasoning
Krazy Salt

Mix all together. Put in greased baking dish. Bake at 350° for 1½ hours. Cover with foil the last hour.

Pinto Beans

2 cups pinto beans

Wash beans and cover with water, bring to boil, turn fire off. Let the beans soak for 2 hours minimum. Drain; rinse beans off. Cover with hot water. Add the following:

Ham bone or 5 slices bacon
¼ cup celery
½ cup fresh tomatoes (not canned)
½ cup bell pepper
1 jalapeño pepper (seeds removed)

¼ cup bacon drippings
4 cloves garlic
Salt to taste
¼ cup onion

Boil till beans are tender.

Really Good Spaghetti

4 cups water
4 tablespoons margarine
1 tablespoon dry onion
1 tablespoon all natural vegetable flakes

1 cup spaghetti
Salt (to taste)

Cook all together till spaghetti is tender, about 10 minutes.

Evelyn's Spam & Spaghetti

1 can Spam (cut in ½-inch squares)
½ cup chopped bell pepper
1 tablespoon garlic and parsley grapeseed oil

½ cup chopped onion
½ cup chopped celery

Dash of the following:
Italian Salad and Dressing Blend Spice   Salt
Seasoning Salt   Nature's Seasons

Sauté the above till onions are clear and Spam is fried. Cook 2 cups spaghetti per package directions; drain. Add Spam mixture to spaghetti, with about 3 tablespoons margarine. Mix and enjoy.

Evelyn's Tamales & Chili Casserole

12 tamales (remove shucks)
¼ chili can of water

1 15-oz. can chili
1 cup shredded Cheddar cheese

Grease casserole bowl; layer the 12 tamales in bowl. Mix the water with the chili and pour over the tamales. Sprinkle the cheese over the chili. Bake at 325° for 25 minutes, till cheese melts.

Evelyn's Pumpkin Casserole

4 cups fresh cooked pumpkin (mashed)
½ cup brown sugar (packed)
2 sm. cans crushed pineapple (drained)
1 cup pecans (chopped)
½ cup marshmallows (miniature)

½ cup sugar
½ teaspoon vanilla
½ cup coconut
1 tablespoon cornstarch
2 tablespoons margarine

Mix well. Cover and bake at 340° for 30 minutes. Serve warm.

Leftover Turkey Casserole

1 cup mayonnaise
2 cups swiss cheese shredded
1 cup celery chopped
¼ cup chopped onion

4 cups turkey chopped up
2 cups croutons
½ cup milk

Put in dish. Bake at 350° for 40 minutes.

Macaroni Casserole

1 cup macaroni
1 can mixed vegetables
Dash of butter and garlic seasoning

¼ cup chopped onion
1 can mushroom soup
Salt and pepper to taste

Simmer the above till done. Put in casserole dish. Add 1 cup grated Cheddar cheese sprinkled on top. Bake at 325° for 10 minutes.

Noodle Casserole

1 6-oz. spinach noodles cooked and drained
1 29-oz. can hominy drained
1 small jar pimientos drained
1 small can mushrooms drained
1 teaspoon Krazy Salt
Dash of pepper and salt

1 stick margarine
1 tablespoon parsley
Dash of Accent
¼ teaspoon Nature's Seasons

Mix the above. Put into casserole bowl. Sprinkle seasoned croutons and 8 oz. shredded Cheddar cheese on top. Bake at 275° for 30 minutes or till cheese melts.

Meal-in-One Pinto Beans Casserole

1 lb. ground meat
1 cup cooked pinto beans
1 egg
1 tablespoon butter (softened)
½ cup flour
1½ teaspoons baking powder

½ cup onion (chopped)
½ cup tomato sauce
¾ cup milk
½ cup yellow cornmeal
1 tablespoon sugar
¼ teaspoon salt

Cook meat with onion till meat is brown and onion is tender. Drain off fat. Add pinto beans. Place mixture in a greased 2-qt. casserole dish. Combine the rest of the ingredients and pour over the meat mixture. Bake at 450° for about 25 minutes or till lightly brown.

Holiday Yams Casserole

2½ lbs. peeled yams (cooked)
1 8½-oz. can crushed pineapple and juice
1 tablespoon butter
½ cup pecans
1 tablespoon brown sugar
1 cup miniature marshmallows

Cook and drain yams and mash well. Stir in rest of ingredients. Spray nonstick spray into a 1½-qt. casserole bowl; spoon in mixture. Bake at 350° for 20 minutes.

Jackie's Cheesy Hashbrown Casserole

1 lb. hashbrowns
¼ cup Velveeta cheese
1 cup cottage cheese (blended)
¾ cup chopped ham
½ cup mushrooms
salt and pepper
¾ cup American cheese
¼ cup mozzarella cheese
1 can mushroom soup
¼ cup green onions (chopped)
¼ stick margarine

Mix the above and pour into a greased casserole dish. Sprinkle 2 cups crushed cornflakes on top. Bake at 350° for about 1 hour.

Eggplant Casserole

1 lb. ground beef
1½ cups chopped peeled eggplant
½ cup tomato sauce
¾ teaspoon ground nutmeg
½ teaspoon garlic powder
¼ cup grated parmesan cheese
Snipped parsley
1 cup chopped onion
1 cup chopped peeled potato
1 teaspoon chili powder
½ teaspoon salt
1 cup plain yogurt
1 egg

Cook meat and onion till brown; drain off fat. Stir in eggplant, potato, tomato sauce, chili powder, nutmeg, salt and garlic powder. Simmer; cover for 20 minutes or till potato and eggplant are tender, and stir in cheese. Spoon into a 1½-qt. casserole dish. Beat egg and yogurt; spoon on top of eggplant mixture. Bake uncovered at 350° for 30 or 35 minutes or till top is set. Sprinkle with parsley.

Cheese Hominy Casserole

1 quart of hominy (drained) ¼ lb. Velveeta cheese (shredded)
Dash of dry Italian Salad Dressing Blend
Dash of dry Onion Dash of Parsley

Combine all ingredients. Put in bowl, sprayed with nonstick spray. Put in microwave, and heat till cheese melts. Stir till well mixed.

Chicken Veggie Casserole

1 cup regular rice	1 fryer cut up
½ cup onion	½ cup bell pepper
1 clove garlic	1 can cream of chicken soup
3 soup cans water	½ cup diced celery
½ cup diced carrots	Salt and pepper

Grease an 8 x 10-inch casserole dish. Spread rice in dish. Fry fryer pieces in pan with oil, just till brown, and place on rice. Sauté onion, bell pepper and garlic. Mix soup and water. Pour all this over chicken and rice. Then sprinkle celery, carrots, salt and pepper on casserole. Cover with lid or foil. Bake at 350° for 45 minutes or till done.

Layer Casserole

Amount of ingredients depends on family size. Layer according to the following, in Pyrex bowl with cover.

1st: hominy
2nd: chopped broccoli
3rd: dot with margarine

Microwave for 7 minutes.

4th: Velveeta cheese
5th: cooked and drained elbow macaroni
6th: Velveeta cheese

Microwave 3 minutes.

Layered Potato Casserole

Layer the following in a greased casserole dish:

slice potatoes
diced onions
diced uncooked bacon
sliced fresh mushrooms
diced bell pepper
top off with another layer of sliced potatoes
dot with butter or margarine
salt and pepper

Bake at 350° till done. Sprinkle with sweet basil.

Salmon Cheese Rice Casserole

1 tablespoon onion	2 stalks celery
½ stick margarine	

Cook above about 3 minutes. Add:

1 tablespoon flour	½ teaspoon salt
Dash of pepper	1 can mushroom soup
¾ cup milk	¼ cup water

Cook all the above into a smooth sauce. Add:

1 cup American cheese (shredded)   1 (15½-oz.) can salmon

Mix all together; put into a greased casserole dish. Top with cracker crumbs. Bake at 350° for about 35 minutes.

Green Bean & Sweet Pea Salad

1 quart drained green beans	1 15½-oz. can sweet peas (drained)
1 small jar pimientos	½ cup celery
¼ cup onion	½ cup bell pepper
1 tablespoon vinegar	½ cup sugar
½ teaspoon Evelyn's Nature's Seasonings (in Special Recipes)	

Mix all together and serve.

Filled Beef Meatloaf Casserole

1 lb. ground beef
½ cup + 1 tablespoon onion (chopped)   2 eggs
½ cup dry bread crumbs   ½ teaspoon pepper
1 teaspoon salt   ½ teaspoon basil

Preheat oven to 350°. Mix the above ingredients. Put ½ of the mixture in a greased loaf pan (9 x 5-inch).

Filling:
1 tablespoon margarine   ¾ cup water
1 teaspoon salt   Dash of pepper
½ cup milk   1¾ cups instant mashed potatoes

Cook the filling till done. Add:

1 beaten egg   ½ cup Cheddar cheese (shredded)

Put on top of meat in pan. Put the other half of meat mixture on top of potato filling. Bake for about 1 hour.

Evelyn's Potato Salad

4 cups potatoes (boiled and cut up)   ½ med. green bell pepper
½ medium yellow pepper   1 small jar pimientos
½ small onion   2 medium pickles
1 stick celery chopped   Dash of Nature's Seasons
Dash of Krazy Salt   2 teaspoons sugar
2 teaspoons walnut oil   Dash of dry dill
Fresh ground black pepper to taste   Salt to taste
1 teaspoon Evelyn's Best Seasoning (in Special Recipes)
Mayonnaise to moisten the above.

Garlic Mushrooms

1 stick margarine melted   1 tablespoon parsley flakes
Dash of salt and pepper   ¼ teaspoon garlic powder
1 lb. mushrooms cut in pieces

Mix the above with the melted margarine, and stir in mushrooms. Cook 6 minutes on level 8 in microwave.

Country Potato Salad

3 large potatoes cooked and cubed
1 large pickle
½ medium bell pepper
Dash of Nature's Seasons
1 teaspoon sugar
1 teaspoon walnut oil
Evelyn's Best Seasoning (in Special Recipes)
Mayonnaise to moisten salad

4 stalks celery
½ medium onion
1 small jar pimentos
Dash of Krazy Salt
Salt and pepper

Mix all together and enjoy. *Hint:* Put it all together (except potatoes) in refrigerator overnight.

Sauerkraut Salad

1 can (16-oz.) sauerkraut (drain, rinse with plain water, drain)
1 cup grated carrots
1 cup chopped green pepper
1 jar 4 oz. pimientos (drained)
½ cup vegetable oil

1 cup chopped celery
1 cup chopped onion
½ cup sugar

Mix ingredients together in large bowl. Let set in refrigerator for 8 hours before serving.

Country Sauerkraut Salad

2½ cups sauerkraut (rinsed and drained real good)
1 large onion chopped
1 small jar pimientos

1 bell pepper cut up
1¾ cups celery

Mix the above together.

Sauce:
1½ cups sugar
¼ cup vinegar

½ teaspoon salt
½ teaspoon celery seed

Pour the sauce over the above. Let set 24 hours.

Green Beans and Garlic

Cook fresh green beans or heat canned green beans and drain.

6 tablespoons margarine or butter   2 cloves garlic (chopped)
Salt to taste

In saucepan heat margarine, garlic and salt. Pour over green beans and stir.

Delicious Lettuce Salad

1 head lettuce   3 sticks celery
2 tomatoes   ½ medium onion
1 medium bell pepper

The above needs ½ cup dressing. Put the following in a measuring cup:

2 tablespoons sugar   ½ teaspoon Krazy Salt
½ teaspoon dry cucumbers   ¾ teaspoon Creole and Cajun
½ teaspoon garlic and herb   ½ teaspoon Nature's Seasons
½ teaspoon walnut oil
1 teaspoon Evelyn's Special Spice (in Special Recipes)

Fill to ½ cup with vegetable oil. Mix and pour over salad.

Vegetable Salad

3 medium cucumbers peeled and sliced   2 medium tomatoes sliced
1 small onion sliced   2 medium bell peppers chopped
¾ cup sugar   1 tablespoon vinegar
Dash of Krazy Salt   Dash of Nature's Seasons

Cucumber Salad 1950

4 cucumbers sliced   1 bell pepper
1 onion   2 tomatoes
3 teaspoons sugar   1 tablespoon vinegar
1 teaspoon avocado oil   1 teaspoon walnut oil
Salt and pepper to taste

Salad Dressing

For ½ cup of salad dressing:

2 tablespoons sugar   ½ teaspoon Krazy Salt
¾ teaspoon Nature's Seasons   ¾ teaspoon Creole and Cajun
½ teaspoon garlic and herb   ½ teaspoon walnut oil
¼ teaspoon Evelyn's Best Seasoning (in Special Recipes)

Fill ½ cup with vegetable oil.

For 1 cup of salad dressing:

4 tablespoons sugar   1 teaspoon Krazy Salt
1½ teaspoons Nature's Seasons   1½ teaspoons Creole and Cajun
1 teaspoon garlic and herb   1 teaspoon walnut oil
½ teaspoon Evelyn's Best Seasoning (in Special Recipes)

Fill cup with vegetable oil

For 1 quart of salad dressing:

1 cup sugar   4 teaspoons Krazy Salt
2 tablespoons Nature's Seasons   2 tablespoons Creole and Cajun
4 teaspoons garlic and herb   4 teaspoons walnut oil
2 teaspoons Evelyn's Best Seasoning (in Special Recipes)

Fill quart with vegetable oil.

For 1 gallon of salad dressing:

4 cups sugar   5 tablespoons+1 teaspoon Krazy Salt
½ cup Nature's Seasons   ½ cup Creole and Cajun
5 tablespoons+1 teaspoon garlic and herb
8 teaspoons Evelyn's Best Seasoning (in Special Recipes)
6 tablespoons walnut oil

Fill gallon with vegetable oil.

Evelyn's Fresh Tomatoes

4 cups fresh tomatoes   ½ cup bell peppers
¼ cup onions   ½ teaspoon Krazy Salt
1 cup sugar   2 tablespoons vinegar
1 teaspoon walnut oil   Dash of garlic and herb
1 teaspoon rosemary vinegar

Sweet Pea Salad

2 cups sweet peas (drained)
3 slices American cheese cut up
Salt and pepper
1 teaspoon parsley flakes
1 tablespoon sugar

1 sm. jar pimientos
3 boiled eggs chopped
Dash Nature's Seasons
2 teaspoons walnut oil
Dash Accent

Stir together. Moisten with mayonnaise.

Evelyn's Rice & Sweet Peas

2 cups sweet peas (drain and save water)
¼ cup rice cooked with margarine and sweet pea water, cool

Add to the above:

1 sm. jar pimientos
½ teaspoon garlic and herbs
Salt and pepper

4 boiled eggs chopped
¼ teaspoon Nature's Seasons
Mayonnaise to moisten

Ranch Macaroni Salad

12 oz. elbow macaroni (cooked, drained, rinsed)
¼ cup chopped onion
½ cup bell pepper
1 pickle
Dash of salt and pepper
2 teaspoons parsley flakes

¾ cup diced tomatoes (fresh)
1 tablespoon sugar
⅛ teaspoon dry dill
Dash of Accent
2 teaspoons walnut oil

Add enough mayonnaise to moisten.

Delicious Potato Soup

½ cup bacon
3 tablespoons vegetable oil
4 cups water
2 carrots
1 small spaghetti squash
4 cups milk
1 teaspoon parsley
8 cups shredded potatoes

1 cup onion
⅛ cup flour
1 medium yellow squash
¼ cup bell pepper
Salt and pepper to taste
1 cup green beans
¼ cup mushrooms

Sauté bacon and onion in vegetable oil. Mix in flour. Add all other ingredients.
Cook on very low heat till done, stirring almost constantly.

Evelyn's Special Chicken Soup

3 quarts water
½ cup chopped onion
½ cup sliced carrots
¼ cup bell pepper
1 cup snow peas
½ teaspoon Nature's Seasons
½ teaspoon soup and vegetable seasoning

9 tablespoons chicken soup base
½ cup corn
½ cup chopped celery
1 chopped potato
¼ teaspoon thyme

Let cook till carrots and potatoes are almost done, then add:

¼ cup elbow macaroni
½ cup egg noodles

¼ cup instant rice

Dumplings

In mixing bowl put 2 eggs. Beat till frothy. Add about 6 to 10 tablespoons flour. Sprinkle with salt and pepper. Mix with spoon till medium thick. While soup is boiling, drop dumplings about a teaspoon at a time. When dumplings come to top of soup, the dumplings are done.

Sweet Potato Surprise

3 sweet potatoes peeled and sliced very thin
3 apples peeled and sliced very thin
¼ cup brown sugar
1 teaspoon maple extract
2 tablespoons butter or margarine
1 cup pecans

1¾ cups whipping cream
2 tablespoons cornstarch
1 teaspoon Danish Pastry extract
2 cups miniature marshmallows

Spray baking dish (8 x 13-inch) with nonstick spray. Mix sweet potatoes, apples, marshmallows and pecans. Put in dish. Blend the whipping cream, cornstarch, butter, extracts and sugar. Pour over potatoes, apples and pecans. Bake at 350° for 20 minutes covered with foil, 20 minutes uncovered, 20 minutes covered with foil, 20 minutes uncovered. Total 80 minutes.

Spaghetti Squash

4 cups cooked squash (about 4 pounds of whole squash) peeled and seeds removed. Cook in microwave (no water added) till tender; drain water. Add:

½ cup margarine   ½ teaspoon salt

Mix the above. And enjoy.

Fancy Fried Okra

Fix a batter of the following:
2 tablespoons dry instant buttermilk	2 teaspoons rosemary vinegar
4 tablespoons flour	1 teaspoon baking powder
Salt and pepper	1 teaspoon dry squash
1 teaspoon Italian salad dressing	1 tablespoon dry onions

Add just enough water to moisten the above.

2 cups okra (cut ½-inch lengths)

Fold okra into above batter; let marinate about 2 hours. Mix 2 cups flour and 2 teaspoons baking powder on a piece of foil. Separate the okra. Place on flour mixture, coat okra. Place on plate till all okra is flour coated. Put about 3 inches of peanut oil in frying pan and heat till very hot. Drop coated okra into oil and fry till golden brown. Don't discard the flour that is left over. Put in bag and freeze till next okra time.

Great Okra

½ lb. bacon cut in strips   ½ cup onion chopped
salt and pepper

Sauté the above till half done.

½ lb. okra (frozen should be rinsed and drained, not thawed)
¾ cup corn meal

Coat okra with corn meal. Add ½ stick margarine. Add to the above and cook on medium heat about 20 minutes covered.

Green Beans and Onions

Cut up onions, fry in small amount vegetable oil. Add to green beans, margarine, and salt, then heat.

Deluxe Country Okra

2 cups okra cut up
1 med. green bell pepper sliced
1¼ cups margarine
1 teaspoon rosemary vinegar
Dash of Italian Salad Dressing Blend
Dash of Evelyn's Dry Marinate Seasoning (in Special Recipes)

½ med. onion sliced
1 small red bell pepper sliced
1 cup water
Dash of salt

Combine all in a pot and cover. Cook slow till okra are tender.

Evelyn's Best Corn

2 cups fresh corn (cut off the cob)
½ cup sugar
¼ cup margarine

Put in baking dish and cover. Put in microwave. Cook for 18 minutes. Stir every 6 minutes.

Squash with Class

Use yellow or spaghetti squash. Fill 2-qt. baking dish with thin-sliced squash. Place ½ cup margarine on top, 2 teaspoons salt; cover baking dish. Put in microwave and bake. As follows: 5 minutes and stir, 4 minutes and stir, test for tenderness.

Saucy Potatoes

½ cup half and half
¼ cup milk
Salt and pepper

½ cup Velveeta cheese
2 tablespoons flour

Dissolve flour in milk; cook the above till thick. Stir in 1 qt. canned potatoes drained. Stir till hot.

Evelyn's Cheese Potatoes

4 cups potatoes sliced ¼-inch thick
Salt and pepper
1 cup longhorn cheese shredded

1 small onion chopped
3 tablespoons margarine

Spray a baking dish with nonstick spray. Combine potatoes, onion, salt and pepper. Place in baking dish, spread margarine on top. Cook in microwave till done, stir every 5 minutes. When done, put cheese on top of potatoes and microwave till cheese melts.

Delicious Canned Potatoes

½ med. onion diced
¼ cup pimiento pepper

½ med. bell pepper
4 tablespoons margarine

Sauté the above until onion is clear. Add 1 qt. drained canned potatoes. Cook and stir till heated.

Zucchini Squash

3 cups diced zucchini squash
2 sticks of celery
½ cup onion
¼ cup margarine
1 teaspoon Italian seasoning
½ teaspoon garlic and herb

1 clove of garlic
2 med. tomatoes peeled and chopped
½ med. bell pepper
½ teaspoon Nature's Seasons
½ teaspoon Krazy Salt
½ teaspoon Creole and Cajun seasoning

Place above ingredients in pot and cover with about a cup of water. Cook till tender, about 30 minutes.

French Fried Okra

1 lb. okra
1½ cups buttermilk

½ teaspoon salt
2 cups self-rising flour

Wash okra and drain well. Cut okra into 1-inch pieces. Sprinkle okra with salt. Add buttermilk, stirring until well coated. Let stand 15 minutes. Drain okra well, coat with flour. Deep fry okra in hot peanut oil 375° until golden brown.

Whipped Cream Mashed Potatoes

6 cups peeled potatoes (cooked)
½ cup margarine
1 tablespoon cream soup base

1 cup whipping cream
Salt and pepper to taste

Add milk, beat all together till fluffy.

Okra Gumbo

2 cups cut okra
½ cup onion
½ teaspoon Italian seasoning
½ teaspoon rosemary vinegar
2 tablespoons bacon grease

¾ cup tomatoes
½ cup bell pepper
2 cloves of garlic
Salt
½ cup margarine

Put all the above in a pot and put water to about half of contents and cook till tender.

Evelyn's Cooked Cabbage

¼ cup bacon drippings
½ cup onion chopped
¼ cup bell pepper chopped
2 cloves garlic chopped

½ cup ham chopped
½ cup carrots chopped
½ cup celery chopped
1 head cabbage

¼ teaspoon of each: flavor enchancer
Krazy Salt
Nature's Seasons

Vegetable Supreme

Sauté the ingredients. Put lid on pot and steam on low heat till tender, about 30 minutes.

Delicious Eggplant

2 tablespoons grapeseed oil (garlic and parsley)
1 tablespoon bacon drippings
½ cup chopped onion
3 cups eggplant (peeled and cut into ½ inch squares)
½ teaspoon chili powder

3 tablespoons margarine
½ cup bell pepper

Dash of salt

Fry onions and bell pepper in above oils. Add eggplant and other spices; cover and slow cook till done.

Evelyn's Garlic Mushrooms

1 stick margarine melted
Dash of salt and pepper
1 lb. mushrooms cut in pieces

1 tablespoon parsley flakes
¼ teaspoon garlic powder

Mix the above with the melted margarine and stir in mushrooms. Cook in microwave, about 6 minutes.

Evelyn's Baked Mashed Potatoes

3 cups (leftover) mashed potatoes
¾ cup onion and garlic croutons, crushed
¾ cup Cheddar cheese, shredded
2 tablespoons margarine or butter
1 tablespoon onion, dry

¼ cup milk
2 eggs beaten
1 teaspoon parsley
¼ teaspoon dry basil
¼ teaspoon dill (dry)

Spray casserole bowl with nonstick spray. Mix all ingredients and place in greased bowl; and cover. Bake at 350° 1 hour.

Meat, Poultry & Seafood

Evelyn's Beef Goulash

1½ lbs. ground meat
½ cup celery
½ cup carrots
⅛ cup chopped fresh parsley
1 can cream of mushroom soup
3 soup cans of water
1 teaspoon browning and seasoning sauce for gravy
Dash of basil, Creole and Cajun, Evelyn's Nature's Seasonings (in Special Recipes)

1 cup diced onion
5 cloves garlic
1 large bell pepper (diced)
Salt and pepper
1 can mushrooms

Brown meat in oil. Add all the rest. Put on lid and steam for 30 minutes.

Judgement Beef BBQ Marinade

Bacon wrap the chunks of meat. Sprinkle the following on the meat:

black pepper
Accent
garlic powder
soy sauce
red pepper

meat tenderizer
seasoning salt
vegetable oil
red wine vinegar

Marinate the meat overnight. Then bar-b-que.

Beef & Vegetables

1 lb. ground meat
4 cloves garlic
1 medium squash
Dash of Creole and Cajun seasoning

½ cup diced onion
½ cup carrots
½ cup bell pepper
Salt and pepper to taste

Brown meat in oil. Add all other ingredients. Steam with lid on very low heat, about 45 minutes.

Roast Beef Tacos

roast (slice paper thin and chop with knife)
onion (chopped up)
salt and pepper

bell pepper (chopped)

In a small amount of shortening sauté onion and bell pepper; add roast and heat.

chopped fresh tomatoes
shredded Cheddar cheese

shredded lettuce
heated flour tortillas

Hearty Spaghetti & Meatballs

1 lb. ground beef
Dash of garlic powder

Salt and pepper

Sauce:
½ lb. breakfast sausage (crumbled)
1 can (6-oz.) tomato paste
2 garlic cloves minced
1 large onion chopped
1 tablespoon beef soup and gravy base
1 tablespoon mushroom soup and gravy base
½ teaspoon of each dried basil, oregano and parsley flakes,
Italian seasoning, garlic and spice, pizza seasoning and cilantro

1 large onion chopped
3 cups tomato puree
Salt and pepper to taste
1 medium green pepper chopped

Hot cooked spaghetti

Grated parmesan cheese

Mix the beef, salt, pepper and garlic powder and make into very small meat-balls. Put in skillet and fry with a little peanut oil till brown. Mix sauce. Put all ingredients in pot and cook on med. Heat for about 30 minutes. Add meatballs to sauce; cook on medium heat for 30 minutes.

Country Steak & Gravy

Coat steak with flour and fry in oil till brown; remove steak. Remove all oil except about 5 tablespoons. Add:

1 med. onion chopped
1 stick of celery
1 cup broccoli

4 cloves garlic
½ cup bell pepper
½ cup red bell pepper

Sauté the above.
Season with:

2 tablespoons Aussie sauce
Salt and pepper
1 teaspoon Creole and Cajun seasoning

1 teaspoon red wine vinegar
1 teaspoon white wine vinegar
1 can mushroom soup

Add the steak on top and simmer for about 1 hour.

Baked Pork Chops

Brown 4 pork chops in oil. Place in baking dish and top with bell pepper, onion, tomatoes, 1 stick margarine, a dash of garlic and herbs spice, and a dash of Nature's Seasons. Bake uncovered at 350° for 45 minutes.

Granny's Pork Chops

Mix all dry ingredients together:

1 teaspoon dry garlic

½ teaspoon dry oregano

1 teaspoon dry onion

½ teaspoon salt

1 teaspoon bread gluten

1 teaspoon Italian salad dressing blend

1 teaspoon of each dry green, yellow and red bell pepper

½ teaspoon dry basil

½ teaspoon dry jalapeño

1 teaspoon sugar

1 tablespoon cornstarch

1 teaspoon dry parsley

Add:

1 tablespoon garlic and parsley grapeseed oil

2 tablespoons original grapeseed oil

⅓ cup water

2 teaspoons rosemary vinegar

Mix all the above together in an ovenproof pan lined with foil and sprayed with nonstick spray. Lay out the pork chops, close together in the pan, and pour the mixture over the chops. Let marinate about 1 hour. Squeeze about a tablespoon of squeezable margarine on top of each chop. Bake at 360° for about an hour or till done.

Bar-B-Que Pork Chops Baked

Brown pork chops in skillet with peanut oil. Lay browned chops in foil-lined baking dish. Sprinkle: brown sugar, dry garlic, dry onion, chili powder, Meat Magic.

On top of chops put a dab of: mustard, tarragon vinegar, Liquid Smoke, teriyaki sauce, soy sauce.

Mix together catsup and tomato sauce, pour on top. Bake at 350° for 1 hour 15 minutes uncovered.

Favorite Broiled Pork Chops

Place pork chops singly in a greased foil-lined pan. Sprinkle seasoned salt, salt and pepper on chops.

Blend in blender: 1 medium sized tomato, 1 medium bell pepper, half medium onion. Pour over chops.

Top with squeezable margarine. Place under broiler, set on low. Broil, turning frequently, for about 40 to 45 minutes.

Granny's Old Time Beef Liver

1. Wash, slice and sprinkle salt and pepper over beef liver, let season.
2. Slice large amount of onion, let stand.
3. In large pot add about 2 inches of water, bring to boil and reduce heat.
4. Add shortening to skillet and heat. Dip liver in flour and brown on both sides. When brown, put in pot with the boiling water; cover.
5. In a skillet put a small amount of shortening and get it hot. Add some flour, and brown in shortening. When brown, add the onions, and fry till clear. Add salt and pepper, put in pot on top of liver. Stir till all is mixed. Cover and put on medium heat; stir about every 3 minutes, just so it doesn't stick to the bottom of the pot. You may have to add more water sometimes. Let steam about 30 minutes.

Meat Loaf

2 lbs. ground beef	2 eggs

Dash of dried onion, garlic, red pepper, celery, tomatoes and basil

1 small jar pimientos	1 can of mushrooms
Salt and pepper to taste	¼ cup regular rice

Mix all the above together. Put in a loaf pan. Bake at 350° for about 1 hour.

Sausage (LR)

25 lbs. meat	⅓ cup black pepper
1 to 1½ teaspoons garlic powder	2 teaspoons red pepper
½ to 1 teaspoons saltpeter	¾ cup salt

Sausage (GL)

100 lbs. meat	
2 lbs. salt	5.5 oz. pepper
2 teaspoons garlic powder	2 teaspoons saltpeter
Deer sausage: ⅓ venison, ⅔ pork	Beef sausage: ½ beef, ½ pork

Best Left Over Roast

Slice roast paper thin and crumble then heat it. Put in warmed flour tortilla. Top with chopped lettuce and tomato and shredded Cheddar cheese.

Stuffed Pork Loin

½ cup fried bacon (chopped)   ½ cup onion
½ cup celery   2 cloves of garlic
1 cup soaked corn bread croutons   Salt and pepper to taste
Dash of cayenne pepper   1 teaspoon garlic and herb spice
Little water to moisten

Mix all the above. Split the pork loin partially to have a flat piece of meat. Spread the filling on the loin. Roll up and tie with string about 1 inch apart. Place in pan on foil. Pour a dab of maple syrup on top of roll. Cover; bake at 350° for about an hour.

Saucy Pork Chops

3 tablespoons garlic and parsley grapeseed oil
2 tablespoons peanut oil   4 pork chops

Coat pork chops with flour. Fry in oils till brown on both sides. Add to the above the following:

½ cup chopped onion   ½ cup celery
½ cup bell pepper   1 teaspoon rosemary vinegar
1 teaspoon ginger and garlic liquid spice   1 cup tomatoes puree
Dash of: Meat Magic, garlic and herbs, Nature's Seasons

Cover frying pan with lid and simmer, about an hour.

Pigs in the Blanket

8 inches of precooked link sausage: Cut in half then cut each half in 4 pieces long ways. Put in microwave 1 or 2 minutes to heat. Drain on paper towel.

1 can of 8 crescent rolls: Roll each piece of sausage in the crescent roll. Bake as directed on can.

Best Pork Chops

Sprinkle the pork chops with the following: Meat Magic, garlic and herb spice, Nature's Seasons, tenderizer, salt and pepper. Let marinate about 1 hour.

In fry pan put 1 tablespoon grapeseed oil (garlic and parsley flavor), 1 tablespoon grapeseed oil (citrus and cilantro flavor). Fry the pork chops till slightly brown. On top of the chops place cut up celery, bell pepper, garlic and onion. Put on the lid and simmer about 1 hour or till tender.

Delicious Ground Beef

1½ lbs. ground beef browned in peanut oil

Add:

1 medium onion	4 bell peppers

Dash of Krazy Salt and Krazy Pepper, garlic powder, parsley flakes

1 small can mushrooms,	1 can mushroom soup

Add water till consistency is satisfactory, and browning and seasoning sauce to color gravy. Cook about 30 minutes on medium heat. Serve over rice.

Hint: *To remove grease from your foods, place 2 lettuce leaves in your pot (example soup or stew). Discard leaves.*

Hint: *To take casing off boiled sausage easier, when finished boiling, quickly pour cold water over sausage.*

Evelyn's Chili

Fry till brown 1½ lbs. ground meat in 2 tablespoons peanut oil. Add:

2 tablespoons masa	2 tablespoons chili powder
1 teaspoon cumin	1 tablespoon chili quik
6 cloves garlic	½ cup onion
¼ cup bell pepper	½ cup fresh tomatoes
1 jalapeño pepper (seeds removed)	Salt and pepper to taste

Sauté all this; slightly add water to cover. Cook till tender.

Marinated & Fried Pork Tenderloin

Slice tenderloin about 1-inch thick and marinate for 3 hours in:

½ teaspoon seasoning salt	Sprig of fresh rosemary
½ teaspoon basil	¼ teaspoon thyme
2 teaspoons onion flakes	1 teaspoon salt
½ teaspoon pepper	Water to cover

Remove tenderloin from marinade. Mix about 2 teaspoons baking powder with flour, dip tenderloin in flour mixture and deep fry, as per the deep fryer instructions.

Pepper Beef Steak

2 lbs. beef round steak cut in strips
4 tablespoons peanut oil
1 cup chopped onion
2 teaspoons sugar
½ teaspoon pepper
½ cup cold water
2 large bell peppers cut in strips
8 oz. canned tomatoes cut up or 2 medium fresh tomatoes

¼ cup soy sauce
3 garlic cloves
½ teaspoon salt
¼ teaspoon ground ginger
1 tablespoon cornstarch

Brown beef in skillet with oil. Put in slow cooker with the next 7 ingredients and cook on low for 5 or 6 hours. Add the tomatoes and bell peppers; cook another 1 hour. Combine the cold water and cornstarch, make a paste. Stir into the liquid in the slow cooker, cook till thick. Serve over noodles or rice.

Barbeque Meatballs

2 lbs. ground meat
3 tablespoons bread crumbs
2 tablespoons dry onion
Add: ½ teaspoon pepper
1 can tomato paste
¼ cup cider vinegar
Diced bell peppers

1⅓ cups ketchup
1 egg
¾ teaspoon garlic salt
1 cup brown sugar
¼ cup soy sauce
1½ teaspoons hot sauce

Preheat oven to 350°. Combine meat, ⅓ cup ketchup, bread crumbs, egg, onion, garlic salt. Mix, shape into 1-inch balls, place on 15 x 10-inch pan, bake 18 minutes or until brown. Transfer meatballs to slow cooker. Mix remaining ingredients. Pour over meatballs. Cover and cook on low 4 hours. Serve with wooden picks. Garnish with bell peppers.

Venison Sausage (Very Hot)

2 lbs. salt
8 oz. garlic (chopped fine)
40 lbs. cured ham

8 oz. black pepper
1 oz. red pepper
60 lbs. pork and 43 lbs. venison

Cola Beef Roast

Season roast as you usually do. Fry roast till brown, put in slow cooker. Add 1 can cola; cook till tender.

Evelyn's Baked Sausage

Take casing off sausage (cut in 1-inch pieces). Lay sausage separately on foil-lined cookie sheet. Pour Italian dressing on top of sausage. Let marinate about 3 hours, turning sausage about every 30 minutes.

Then line a 13 x 8-inch pan with foil. Put a cake cooling rack on top of pan, and place sausage on top of rack. Bake at 375° for 45 minutes.

The reason for the rack on top of the pan is the liquid from the sausage drains, and the sausage gets nice and brown.

Pork Spare Ribs

Sprinkle the following on the spare ribs:
Evelyn's Dry Marinade and Seasoning (in Special Recipes)
Italian salad dressing seasoning   Salt and pepper
All purpose seasoning   Garlic and herbs
Meat tenderizer

Put the above in skillet with ¼ cup bacon drippings. Fry till brown. On top of spare ribs add:

½ cup onions chopped   ½ teaspoon garlic flakes
4 bay leaves   1 cup fresh snow peas
½ cup water

Cover skillet; cook on medium heat for about 1 hour.

Fried Pork Chops

4 pork chops   ½ teaspoon dry red bell pepper
½ teaspoon dry garlic   ½ teaspoon dry celery
½ teaspoon dry onion   Salt and pepper

Mix together and sprinkle over pork chops. Let set 1 hour. Dip chops in flour and fry.

Timmermann Family Venison Sausage

50 lbs. meat: ½ venison, ½ pork   14 to 16 oz. salt (canning salt)
3 oz. black pepper (coarse)   2 teaspoons red pepper
1 teaspoon saltpeter   1 bulb garlic (fresh cut up fine)

Make a meat patty and fry it. Test seasoning for your taste.

Evelyn's Beef or Pork Marinade

About 1 teaspoon of each of the dry ingredients. Minimum depends on the amount of meat to be marinated (use judgement):

brisket rub	Creole and Cajun seasoning
Salad Supreme seasoning	flavor enchancer
garlic powder	dry jalapeño
Nature's Seasons	meat tenderizer
grill seasoning	ginger
Cajun seasoning	Meat Magic
frijoles seasoning	soup and vegetable spice
chili powder	garlic and herb spice
garlic pepper blend	pinch of herbs

Add about 3 tablespoons of the following:

tarragon vinegar	balsamic vinegar
red vinegar	rosemary vinegar
vidalia onion dressing	garlic oil
garlic juice	lemon juice
vegetable oil	garlic and parsley grapeseed oil

About 2 cups of each of the following:

teriyaki	soy sauce

Mix all the above: let marinate 24 hours. Turn meat in marinade every 2 hours. Put on Bar-B-Q pit.

Mop ingredients: 3 cups pineapple juice, 1 cup lemon juice, ½ cup margarine, ½ cup vegetable oil. Heat in pan just till margarine melts. Mop meat every 10 minutes.

Cook on pit 3 hours, wrap meat in foil. Bake at 365° for 4 hours till very tender, then sit back and enjoy all your hard labor.

The Best Fried Chicken

Place in bowl:

4 chicken thighs	½ teaspoon garlic and spice
½ teaspoon cayenne pepper	2 tablespoons salt (no mistake)
1 teaspoon Nature's Seasons	1 teaspoon meat tenderizer

Sprinkle the above on the chicken; cover chicken with tap water. Marinate for 3 hours. Drain. Put peanut oil in deep fryer set at 325°. Mix 2 cups flour with 1 ½ teaspoons baking powder and sprinkle of pepper. Coat chicken pieces with flour. Dip chicken pieces in milk. Coat chicken pieces with flour. Put chicken pieces in deep fryer at 325° for 12 to 15 minutes.

1899 Recipe for Tamales

Meat:

pork or deer	beef and pork

Boil meat with water, salt and bacon grease. Boil till done, drain (save liquid). Cool and grind meat. Add to meat the following:

onion	garlic (chop real fine)
salt	pepper
paprika	chili powder
comino	cayenne pepper
bacon grease	chili quik

Mix and taste to your specifications. Soak your shucks overnight in water. Mix masa with some of the drained liquid.

salt	lard

Make it so you can spread it on the shucks. Add meat mixture and roll up. Put tamales in colander. Set into a large pot and add enough water just to reach bottom of colander. Cook about 3 to 3½ hours, just simmering. Watch so water doesn't boil out. You will have to add more water. 6 pounds of meat to 5 pounds of masa makes about 138 tamales.

Never Forget Fried Turkey

14-lb. turkey injected with 3 cups of marinade, as follows:
1½ cups bottled marinate garlic and herb (not Creole type)
1½ cups bottled marinate garlic and butter

Rub turkey inside and out with ground fresh black pepper and salt. Put in large plastic bag and marinate for 24 hours. To fry a 14-lb. turkey, 3½ gallons of peanut oil in a 28-quart pot. Fry at 325° for 1 hour or till thigh reaches 180 degrees.

Jalapeño Chicken Supreme

6 chicken thighs	½ cup jalapeño jelly
3 tablespoons vegetable oil	2 teaspoons lemon juice
1 teaspoon garlic salt	1 teaspoon lemon pepper
2 teaspoons chili powder	1 teaspoon dry bell pepper

Put in 15 x 11-inch pan lined with foil and spray with nonstick cooking spray. Arrange chicken in single layer. Bake at 400° for 18 minutes. Drain juices. Combine the last 7 ingredients. Baste chicken on both sides. Bake 18 minutes. Turn chicken. Baste with rest of sauce. Bake for 15 minutes or till done.

Evelyn's Baked Turkey

Turkey cut in ½, sprinkled with the following:

celery salt	parsley
marjoram	sage
Evelyn's Nature's Seasonings (in Special Recipes)	
Krazy Salt	rosemary
garlic and herb	garlic and pepper
salt	pepper

Put turkey in roaster. Put vegetable oil and soft margarine over the turkey and a little water in roaster. Bake at 350° till tender.

Evelyn's Fried Turkey

Put the following in blender and inject turkey with needle.

1 med. onion	2 garlic cloves
1 stalk celery	1 medium bell pepper
Dash of cayenne pepper	Salt and pepper

Marinate for 1 day. In a 28-quart pot heat 3½ gallons peanut oil to 325°; put in turkey. Turkey has to be covered with hot oil. Cook 14-lb. turkey for 1 hour, 9-lb. turkey for 27 minutes. Cook to 180 degrees (thigh is best to check).

Country Chicken Cacciatore

1½ lbs. diced chicken	2 tablespoons olive oil
¾ cup sliced onions	¼ cup celery chopped
½ cup bell pepper sliced	½ teaspoon basil
½ teaspoon garlic and herbs	Salt and pepper to taste
2 medium fresh tomatoes (peeled and chopped)	

Spray skillet with nonstick spray, add the oil. Put in the chicken and fry till golden brown. Remove the chicken. Put in the onions, celery and peppers, sauté till tender. Put in the tomatoes and spices. Add the chicken. Cook over medium heat about 10 minutes, till chicken is done. Put in baking dish. Sprinkle shredded parmesan cheese over chicken. Put in oven till cheese melts. Serve over cooked spaghetti.

Evelyn's Jalapeño Spice Blend Chicken

Coat chicken pieces with the Jalapeño Spice Blend (in Special Recipes). Then coat chicken pieces with cornflake crumbs. Put in a foil-lined pan sprayed with nonstick spray. Pat top of chicken with margarine. Bake at 350° till tender. Don't turn pieces over.

Chicken Sautey

1 fryer cut up
½ cup peanut butter
1 teaspoon garlic
2 teaspoons chili powder

½ cup catsup
¼ cup lime juice
1 teaspoon cayenne
Dash soy sauce

Marinate in the above for about 4 hours. Then grill till done.

Evelyn's Baked Chicken & Rice

Use chicken breast or thighs or whatever you want. Mix the following dry spices together, sprinkle over chicken:

cilantro
garlic and herb
Evelyn's Nature's Seasonings (in Special Recipes)
garlic and spice

grill seasoning
garlic peppercorns

thyme

Pour the following ingredients in foil-lined pan

liquid ginger and garlic
grapeseed oil citrus and cilantro

liquid lemon and dill seasoning

Layer chicken in pan. Put sliced onion, sliced green, red and yellow bell pepper on top of chicken. Bake at 350° uncovered till dry, then cover and cook till tender. Then uncover and remove chicken. Put rice in the juices and chicken on top of the rice. Cover; put back in the oven and bake till the rice is tender.

Pete Krause Orange Baked Turkey

Prepare turkey to your specifications or use recipe. Peel oranges and leave whole, with fork punch holes all around the orange. Stuff the turkey cavity tight with the oranges. Bake as usual. You will have the juiciest turkey and no orange taste.

T.V. Grilled Chicken

1 fryer

With scissors cut the back of the fryer, split open. Cut the breast bone, and pull out. Flatten out fryer like a butterfly. Loosen the skin by running your fingers under it.

peppercorns (grind in coffee mill)	parsley
fresh lemon	salt
garlic	

Add enough olive oil to make paste. With a spoon put the paste under the fryer skin and rub with hands to smooth paste under fryer skin. Cut in chunks the following: carrots, onions and celery. Put in roasting pan, lay fryer on top of vegetables with skin side up. Put in oven set on grill, for about 20 minutes or till skin is brown. Turn fryer cut-side up, and bake about 10 minutes. Make sure meat reaches 165°.

Evelyn's Divine Chicken

4 chicken breasts or your favorite chicken parts

Sprinkle with dry cilantro or use fresh salt and pepper. Line pan with foil and spray with nonstick spray. Place chicken in pan. On top of chicken put the following:

1 med. green bell pepper	1 med. yellow bell pepper
1 med. red bell pepper	1 med. onion

Add

3-inch stalk fresh rosemary	garlic butter

Fold the foil over the above ingredients to make it airtight. Bake at 350° for 1 hour 15 minutes; open foil and remove chicken. Stir in 1 cup instant rice. Place chicken on top of rice. Put back into oven about 10 minutes. Delicious.

Country Time Chicken

Sprinkle chicken pieces with Evelyn's Marinade and Seasoning (in Special Recipes) and let marinate about 2 hours. Line baking pan with foil sprayed with nonstick spray.

Mix 2 cups cornflake crumbs and ½ cup Cajun style fish fry readi-mix, and coat chicken on both sides and lay pieces as close together as possible. After all the pieces are coated spread a generous amount of squeezable margarine over all. Bake at 350° for 1½ hours uncovered. About every 20 minutes squeeze more margarine over chicken.

Evelyn's Cornmeal Mix to Coat Chicken

1 cup flour
1 teaspoon cumin
1 teaspoon salt
2 teaspoons garlic powder
1 teaspoon poultry seasoning
1 teaspoon Evelyn's Nature's Seasonings (in Special Recipes)

1 cup cornmeal
2 teaspoons onion powder
½ teaspoon pepper
½ teaspoon dry rosemary

In airtight container combine the first 10 ingredients. Store in a cool dry place. Makes about 2¼ cups, enough for 3 batches additional ingredients

1 fryer (about 3 lbs) cut up and skinned
4 tablespoons butter (melted)

Place ¾ cup of mix in plastic bag. Dip chicken in melted butter. Add chicken to plastic bag and shake to coat. Place in a greased 15 x 10 x 1-inch pan and bake uncovered 375° for 45 to 50 minutes or till done.

Evelyn's Finger Licking Chicken

Marinate in the following for about 6 hours 1 fryer. All dry ingredients:
½ teaspoon cilantro
1 teaspoon celery salt
½ teaspoon marjoram
½ teaspoon sage
1 ½ teaspoons parsley
1 teaspoon Nature's Seasons
1½ teaspoons Krazy Salt
¾ teaspoon dry jalapeño
1 teaspoon garlic and herb

1 teaspoon dry onion
1 teaspoon dry red bell pepper
1 teaspoon dry bell pepper
1 teaspoon dry dill
1 teaspoon dry celery
1 teaspoon dry mustard

½ teaspoon rosemary
Salt and pepper to taste

Rub on chicken to marinate. Rotisserie or bake at 350° for 1½ hours till tender.

Evelyn's Fancy Baked Turkey

Sprinkle the turkey with the following:
celery salt
marjoram
Nature's Seasons
rosemary
garlic and pepper spice

parsley
sage
Krazy Salt
garlic and herb spice
salt and pepper

Let marinate for 2 hours. Place turkey in foil with ¼ cup vegetable oil and ½ cup margarine. Wrap turkey completely in foil and seal; place in pan. Bake at 350° (time depends on size of turkey). Baste about every 45 minutes.

Marinated & Baked Turkey Breast

¼ cup canning salt
1 teaspoon celery salt
1 teaspoon cayenne pepper

1 teaspoon garlic flakes
Water
1 teaspoon Creole and Cajun seasoning

Mix the above in large pot. Put in breast and cover with water. Marinate for 3 hours or more. Drain and sprinkle the following. Mix:

1 teaspoon garlic and spice
1 teaspoon Evelyn's Nature's Seasonings (in Special Recipes)
1 teaspoon meat tenderizer
1 teaspoon salt

1 teaspoon poultry seasoning

½ teaspoon pepper

Drain breast and put in foil-lined roaster. Rub the above over breast. Bake at 350° for about 3 hours or until tender.

Note: *To know when the oil is perfectly hot for frying seafood. When you put oil in the pan, drop in a match. When the match lights (it goes out right away) remove the match. Start frying the seafood.*

Evelyn's Shrimp Toast

shrimp
cayenne pepper
salt

onion
parsley

Put the above in food processor. Spread on slices of bread with bread crust removed and fry in skillet.

Evelyn's Grilled Catfish Marinade

6 (4-oz.) catfish fillets
¼ cup lemon juice
½ teaspoon pepper
½ teaspoon Creole or Cajun seasoning

¼ cup soy sauce
½ teaspoon garlic salt
⅛ teaspoon lemon pepper

Mix all together and lay catfish in marinade. Marinate for 1 hour in refrigerator. Drain fish. Lay fish in pan. Cut 1 stick of margarine. Lay on top of fish. Grill fish till it flakes, about 15 or 20 minutes

Whipped Butter 1975

1 lb. soft margarine whipped
½ teaspoon butter flavor

1 small can evaporated milk (⅔ cup)

Great for dipping shrimp or fish.

Special Tartar Sauce

1 pint mayonnaise
¼ cup chopped onion
¼ teaspoon ground mustard
½ stalk celery chopped

1 cup sweet pickle relish
¼ teaspoon pepper
1 teaspoon sugar
⅛ teaspoon Worcestershire sauce

Blend all ingredients and refrigerate.

Crab or Shrimp Boil Spice

4 tablespoons pickling spice
1 teaspoon dry cilantro
¼ teaspoon celery seed
1 tablespoon bay leaf (broken up)
1 teaspoon garden vegetable snacks and dip seasoning

1 tablespoon dry dill
1 teaspoon dry mustard
1 tablespoon royal peppercorns

Mix all together and put in airtight bottle. *To use:* Put in spice ball and hang on pot to boil crab legs or shrimp.

Seafood Boiling Pot Sensation

No measurements in this recipe because I have no idea of how many you are cooking for. Plus you may add more of what you like. Large pot with enough water to cover the following:

fresh whole potatoes
fresh parsley sprigs
Cajun seasoning (to taste)

fresh onions
bell pepper
salt

Cook the above 15 minutes.

Add: Corn on the cob (ear corn only; fresh cobs have lots of flavoring) and fresh country sausage after it has been cut in chunks and fried in a small amount of vegetable oil till brown. Cook 15 minutes.

Add: Shrimp, cook 5 minutes. Don't overcook, make sure the potatoes are still firm. *Optional:* garlic and bay leaf.

Beer Batter for Shrimp or Fish Fillets

¼ cup vegetable oil
1 cup flour
¼ teaspoon salt

1 egg beaten
¾ teaspoon seasoned salt
½ teaspoon baking powder

Add beer to thin batter to dipping consistency.

Butterfly Shrimp

3 dozen shrimp
1 teaspoon salt
1 teaspoon baking powder
1 cup water

1 teaspoon garlic juice
1½ cups flour
½ cup salad oil
Peanut oil

Shell shrimp. Split tops and flatten for a butterfly shape. Place in a shallow pan. Add garlic juice and ½ teaspoon salt. Mix well. Set aside for 1 hour to blend flavors.

In small bowl mix flour, salt and baking powder. Add oil little at a time, stirring until mixture leaves sides of bowl. Gradually add water; mix until well blended and smooth. Dip shrimp in batter. Deep fry in oil heated to 375° to 400° until golden brown on both sides, about 3 minutes.

Evelyn's BBQ Salmon Marinade

Marinate for 2 hours
1 teaspoon lemon pepper
½ teaspoon of each of the following:

dry onion	dry garlic	dry bell pepper
chili powder	salt	dry parsley
corn syrup	garlic and herb	mustard
Krazy Salt	dry celery	Magic Season blends

¼ cup soy sauce
½ cup vegetable oil
3 lbs. salmon
Dash of Creole and Cajun seasoning

¼ cup margarine
¼ cup teriyaki sauce
Dash of garlic and pepper blend
¼ cup grapeseed oil garlic and parsley

Then Bar-B-Q! Baste fish with ¼ cup lemon juice, ½ cup vegetable oil and ¼ cup margarine. Baste it every time you check salmon.

Texas Broiled Salmon

slab of salmon

Mix together ¼ to ½ teaspoon of each (what you like more of, put more of):
Evelyn's Nature's Seasonings (in Special Recipes)

lemon pepper	Fiesta seasoning
garlic and herb	thyme
garlic and spice	pepper ranch
pizza seasoning	Creole and Cajun seasoning
Krazy Salt	fresh cracked pepper
dry onion	dry mustard
garlic salt	dry butter seasoning
seasoning salt	

Rub into salmon slab. Let marinate 2 to 6 hours. Place on foil-lined pan that has been sprayed with nonstick spray. Pour lemon juice around salmon, just till it tops the salmon. Then slice margarine and place on top of salmon. Put under the broiler on low setting for 35 minutes. Baste every 5 minutes with the juice on side of salmon. After 35 minutes scrape the seasoning off the salmon and pour off all the juice out of the pan and pour in enough water to reach the top of the salmon; broil for 5 minutes. Baste and cook 5 minutes more and enjoy!

Country Broiled Catfish

¼ cup lemon juice   ¼ cup soy sauce

Sprinkle of each:

salt	garlic and herb
Nature's Seasons	lemon pepper
garlic and spice	Cajun spice

Mix all the above and pour over catfish that has been put in a foil-lined pan. Marinate about 1 hour; drain. Take 1 stick margarine cut into long strips. Lay on top of fish. Put under broiler. Baste about every 5 minutes with the juices around the fish. Broil about 20 or 30 minutes till cooked.

Ranch Tartar Sauce

1 tablespoon ranch dressing mix (in Special Recipes)
⅓ cup mayonnaise   ⅓ cup sour cream
3 tablespoons sweet pickle relish

Blend dressing with mayonnaise, sour cream, and the pickle relish. Chill 1 hour. Makes 1 cup.

Evelyn's Salmon Drops

¼ lb. saltine crackers
3 eggs
3 sticks celery
Dash of Evelyn's Special Spice (in Special Recipes)

15-oz. can of salmon (drained)
¼ medium onion
Dash of dry dill

Put all ingredients in food processor and process till smooth. Drop from spoon into skillet with hot peanut oil.

Evelyn's Sand Trout

Spray nonstick spray in foil-lined pan. Place the sand trout on the foil. Sprinkle salt, pepper, dry dill, lemon pepper on both sides of fish. Sprinkle lemon and dill, liquid spice, and grapeseed oil on both sides. Put margarine on top of fish. Bake at 350° for 40 minutes, turning once at half time.

Country Cooked Shrimp

1 or 1½ lbs. shrimp, cleaned and deveined
1 large carrot (about ¼-inch slices)
1 med. onion sliced
Dash of salt
Dash of Evelyn's Nature's Seasonings (in Special Recipes)
Dash of Evelyn's Dry Marinade Seasoning (in Special Recipes)

4 stalks celery (about ¼-inch slices)
1 cup water
Dash of Italian salad dressing blend

Put all ingredients in a pot, cover and cook slow till vegetables are tender. Mix 1 tablespoon cornstarch in a small amount of water. Add a small amount at a time; add till it is thick enough. Serve over cooked rice.

Delicious Broiled Catfish

Line pan with foil. Spray with nonstick spray. Place fish on foil. Sprinkle with Krazy Salt and lemon pepper. Slice margarine sticks in four long ways and place over fish. Let set approximately 1½ hours on top of stove. Place under broiler for about 15 or 20 minutes or till it flakes.

Evelyn's Broiled Salmon with Rub

slab of salmon (8 x 4-inch)

½ teaspoon of each:
lemon pepper	Krazy Salt
Evelyn's Nature's Seasonings (in Special Recipes)	
garlic and herb	thyme
garlic and spice	pepper ranch
pizza seasoning	paprika
Creole and Cajun seasoning	dry bell pepper
dry onion	dry jalapeño

¼ cup teriyaki	¼ cup soy sauce
¼ cup vegetable oil	1 tablespoon cracked pepper

Marinate salmon in the last 4 ingredients about 1 hour; drain. Mix the dry ingredients. Coat salmon on both sides. Put salmon in foil-lined pan, sprayed with nonstick spray. Put some sliced stick butter on salmon. Baste it every time you check it. Broil on high till tender, about 15 or 20 minutes or till it flakes.

Evelyn's Catfish Marinade

¾ teaspoon lemon pepper	1 tablespoon dry onion
1 tablespoon dry bell pepper	½ teaspoon dry garlic
½ teaspoon salt	½ teaspoon chili powder
1 cup soy sauce	1 cup teriyaki sauce
3 lbs. catfish	½ teaspoon Creole and Cajun seasoning

Marinate for 2 hours. Put on bar-b-que pit mop with: peanut oil, margarine, lemon juice. Cook till done.

Evelyn's Salmon Patties

1 15-oz. can salmon (drained)	¼ lb. saltine crackers (crushed)
1 egg	

Mix the 3 ingredients together. Make into patties. Put in skillet with hot oil and fry till brown on both sides.

Broiled King Fish

Sprinkle king fish with the following:

Creole seasoning

lemon pepper

Krazy Salt

Italian salad dressing blend seasoning

garlic and herb seasoning

Marinate for 2 hours. Put in pan, put margarine on top of fish and broil till done.

Evelyn's Fried Shrimp

30 shrimp

Marinate with the following:

3 eggs

1 tablespoon dry dill

1 tablespoon rosemary vinegar

1½ teaspoons lemon and dill spice

Sprinkle with salt and pepper. Blend the marinade well. Add shrimp. Let set about 3 hours. Drain. Coat the shrimp with flour and deep fry. *Caution:* You will not want to share them.

Boiled Shrimp

3 cups water

3 bay leaves

1 teaspoon dry garlic

Shrimp

3 tablespoons pickling spice

3 teaspoons dry onion

1 teaspoon salt

Boil the above together, add the cleaned shrimp. Boil 5 minutes. Cut off heat and let shrimp set in hot brine for 10 minutes.

Best Country Broiled Salmon

Piece of fresh salmon about 6 x 6-inch

Place in a foil-lined pan, sprayed with nonstick spray. Sprinkle the following on top of salmon:

1 tablespoon lemon

Dash of dry dill

1 teaspoon Evelyn's Dry Marinade Spice (in Special Recipes)

1 teaspoon Evelyn's Nature Seasoning (in Special Recipes)

½ teaspoon Italian salad dressing blend   ½ teaspoon salsa seasoning

Let marinate about 30 minutes. Spread squeezable margarine on top and put under broiler and broil till done, about 30 minutes.

Evelyn's Spaghetti Shrimp

24 shrimp
12 toes of garlic (no mistake)   ½ cup margarine

Sauté the above just till the flavors blend. Add:

12 oz. frozen broccoli (cut up) to the shrimp
Dash of Creole and Cajun seasoning

Cook 1½ cups dry spaghetti in another pot till about ¾ done. Drain some of the liquid. Add the spaghetti to the shrimp and cook till spaghetti is done. Add salt to taste, and you may want to add more margarine.

Seafood Tip: *Soak fish in chopped watermelon to remove the fishy smell.*

Special Recipes
& Substitutions

Special Beer Batter

The bubbles in the beer give you a crisp topping. Make a batter for beef, pork, chicken and seafood.

1 cup flour	¼ cup buttermilk
½ cup beer	Salt and pepper

Blend the above till smooth. Dip your choice of meat in batter, then in corn meal or flour. In batter again. Then in corn meal or flour again. Put in hot oil and fry.

Beef, Veggies & Seafood Batter

1 cup flour	1 egg
1 cup ice water	2 tablespoons oil
½ teaspoon sugar	½ teaspoon salt

Blend together, coat the food and fry.

Aunt Ora's Coated Cheetos

Bake 14 oz. Cheetos at 250° for 1 hour, stirring every 15 minutes. Melt the following:

1 cup sugar	1 cup brown sugar
½ cup white corn syrup	3 sticks butter

Pour over Cheetos and stir, and separate.

Evelyn's Piña Colada Punch 50's

46 oz. can pineapple juice	16 oz. cream of coconut
1 quart vanilla ice cream	28 oz. 7-Up

Mix together and enjoy.

Texas Apple Pie Shake Beverage

1 can condensed milk	1¼ cups applesauce
½ cup apple juice	½ teaspoon apple pie spice
3 cups crushed ice	

Put all the above in blender. Serve immediately.

Egg Nog Drink

3 cups whipping cream
1 cup sugar
1½ cups whiskey (your option)

3 cups milk
6 eggs

Put all together in blender. Serve with a dash of nutmeg.

Tudyk Bologna Spread or Dip

1 lb. bologna
1 medium onion

1 medium dill pickle

Grind all 3 ingredients in food grinder. Moisten with mayonnaise. Makes delicious sandwiches or dip.

Evelyn's Cheese Dip (Little Warm)

3 lbs. Velveeta cheese (cut in chunks)
1 lb. Velveeta Mexican cheese (cut in chunks)
1 small jar pimientos

Sauté the 3 following ingredients:

½ cup bacon cut in slivers
½ cup onion
Dash of Nature's Seasons

½ cup bell pepper
1 cup milk
Dash of Italian seasoning

Mix all the above. Cook very slow and stirring till all is melted.

Shrimp Ball Dip

8-oz. cream cheese
1 teaspoon mustard
12 shrimp cooked and cut up

1 teaspoon lemon
1 tablespoon onion
Pecans

Mix all except pecans. Mix and roll into a ball. Coat with pecans.

BBQ Cheese Ball or Log

8 oz. cream cheese (soften)   1 tablespoon BBQ sauce concentrate

Mix well. Mound in center of plate or make into a log. Garnish with omelette soufflé seasoning. Cover and chill overnight. Serve with crackers.

Texas Shrimp Dip

1 can cream of mushroom soup (10¾ oz.)
8-oz. cream cheese   1 cup fresh boiled shrimp
½ cup of each chopped celery, green onion
¼ cup mayonnaise   ¼ teaspoon dill

Beat well mushroom soup, cream cheese and mayonnaise. Stir in shrimp, celery and green onion. Put in bowl. Serve with crackers or vegetables.

Seafood Avocado Dip

1 (6-oz.) can tuna   1 large avocado peeled and mashed
3 teaspoons lemon juice   3 cloves garlic (mashed)
1 tablespoon grated onion   1 jalapeño pepper chopped

Mix all together. Serve with assorted crackers.

South Texas Shrimp Dip

1 cup boiled shrimp   1½ cups chopped tomatoes
1 large avocado peeled and mashed   1 jalapeño chopped
½ cup onion chopped   ¼ cup cilantro chopped
2 teaspoons lemon juice   2 cloves garlic chopped

Combine all together. Serve with chips.

Evelyn's Salmon Dip or Spread

2 cups canned salmon   3 sticks celery chopped fine
1 tablespoon onion chopped fine   Dash of Nature's Seasons
Italian salad dressing blend   Mayonnaise to moisten

Enjoy with crackers. Makes a delicious sandwich.

Cucumber Cream Cheese Dip

8-oz. cream cheese   ¾ cup peeled grated cucumber
3 tablespoons green onion   Dash of cayenne pepper and salt

Blend together. If too thick add some mayonnaise. Serve with chips or crackers.

Cheese and Ham Dip

1 cup mayonnaise
2 jars pimento cheese spread
2 tablespoons chopped green onion
2 small cans deviled ham
4 tablespoons chopped parsley
5 drops hot sauce

Mix all together. Beat with mixer.

Evelyn's Ranch Chip or Salad Mix

2 tablespoons salt
2½ teaspoons MSG
1½ teaspoons garlic powder
1½ teaspoons pepper
4 teaspoons parsley flakes
1½ teaspoons onion powder

Mix the above ingredients. Store the dry mixture in airtight container in refrigerator until ready to use.

#1 Plain Ranch:
1½ cups mayonnaise
1½ cup buttermilk
3½ teaspoons Evelyn's Ranch Chip or Salad Mix

Blend the 3 above ingredients. Stir well before serving.

Creamy Herb: Add the following to #1:
1½ tablespoons chopped chives
1 toe garlic (crushed)
½ teaspoon dry tarragon

Creamy Italian: Add the following to #1:
Dash of cayenne pepper
1½ teaspoons Italian seasoning

Spaghetti Mix

¼ cup cornstarch
¼ cup dry parsley
2 tablespoons dry Italian seasoning
4 teaspoons sugar
¼ cup dry onion
3 tablespoons dry bell pepper
4 teaspoons salt
2 teaspoons dry garlic

Combine ingredients. Store in airtight container in a cool dry place. Additional ingredients:

1 lb. ground beef
1 6-oz. can tomato paste
2 cups water

In skillet brown beef, drain. Stir in ¼ cup mix, water and tomato paste. Bring to boil. Boil and stir 2 minutes. Reduce heat and simmer for 20 minutes.

Ranch Dressing Mix Plus

½ cup finely crushed saltine crackers (about 15)
½ cup dry onion   1 cup dry parsley
½ cup garlic salt   ½ cup onion salt
¼ cup garlic powder   ¼ cup onion powder
3 tablespoons dry dill

Combine all ingredients and put in airtight container. Store in cool place. Additional ingredients:

For Ranch Dressing:
2 cups mayonnaise   2 cups buttermilk
3 tablespoons mix Ranch Dressing Mix Plus

Whisk together and refrigerate. Yield 4 cups.

For Thousand Island Dressing:
1 cup prepared ranch dressing   ¼ cup chili sauce
3 tablespoons sweet pickle relish

For Cucumber Dressing:
1 cup prepared ranch dressing   1 teaspoon celery seed
1 medium cucumber peeled, seeded and puréed

Evelyn's Delicious Popcorn Balls

Mix together:
5 qts. popped popcorn   1½ cups chopped pecans

Then in saucepan combine the following:
1 cup white corn syrup   3 tablespoons butter
1 cup brown sugar   1½ cups white sugar
1 teaspoon vanilla nut extract   1 teaspoon vanilla
1 teaspoon butter pecan extract

Cook till soft ball stage. While hot pour over popcorn and pecans and stir till all is coated. Spread out on greased foil. Cool. Make into balls.

Cranberry Sauce

1 cup fresh cranberries   ½ cup water
½ cup sugar

Put water and sugar in pot and bring to boil, then add cranberries. Cook for about 7 minutes. Pour in bowl to cool.

The Best Sweet Rice

1 cup regular rice
4 cups milk

¼ teaspoon salt
1 cup sugar

Put rice, salt and 3 cups milk in double boiler; let cook for 30 minutes over medium heat. Stir occasionally with fork. Add 1 cup sugar and 1 cup milk; let cook another 20 to 30 minutes until firm. Pour in bowl; let cool. Sprinkle with sugar and cinnamon.

Sweetened Condensed Milk

⅓ cup water
3 tablespoons margarine
¾ cup dry milk

⅓ cup non-dairy creamer
⅔ cup sugar
Dash of salt

Combine water and margarine; bring to boil. Add rest of ingredients. Stir well. Put in blender to mix.

Butter Topping

1 stick margarine
¼ teaspoon seasoning salt

¼ teaspoon lemon pepper
1 teaspoon parsley

Put on vegetables, chicken or seafood.

Rosemary Vinegar

Pack a quart bottle with fresh cut-up rosemary stems. Pour white 5% vinegar over rosemary till bottle is full. Let stand about a week. Enjoy over meats, seafood and vegetables.

Toasted Pumpkin Seed

When removed from pumpkin separate seed from holding and wash. Put seed in bowl. Take paper towels and swish in seed to dry seed. Lightly pour grape-seed oil (original) over seeds and sprinkle with salt. Put foil in 13 x 9 x 2-inch pan and spray with nonstick spray. Pour seed in and stir about every 10 minutes. Roast at 250° in oven for about 2 hours.

Evelyn's Salad Spice

(This recipe will be for cooks who dehydrate vegetables.)

¼ cup dry bell pepper
⅛ cup dry celery
¼ cup dry yellow squash
¼ cup dry cucumbers
¼ cup dry parsley

⅛ cup dry red bell pepper
¼ cup dry spaghetti squash
¼ cup dry pumpkin
⅛ cup dry dill
¼ cup dry onion

Put in blender to mix completely. Use on any food. Put in cabbage slaw, potato salad, lettuce salad and fish.

Evelyn's Special Spice

½ teaspoon dry garlic
1 teaspoon dry dill

1 teaspoon dry onion
¼ teaspoon dry jalapeño

Put on salads, potatoes, etc.

Evelyn's Gourmet Seasoning

2 tablespoons dry onion
1 tablespoon salt
1 teaspoon garlic peppercorns
1 teaspoon dry red bell pepper
½ teaspoon cayenne pepper
½ teaspoon white pepper
1 teaspoon sweet basil
½ teaspoon oregano
1½ teaspoons Italian salad dressing blend

1 tablespoon dry garlic
1 tablespoon garlic salt
1 tablespoon garlic and spice
2 teaspoons dry mustard
1 tablespoon parsley
1 teaspoon black pepper
4 bay leaves
½ teaspoon thyme

Blend together in blender. Use on all meats, vegetables, soups and casseroles.

Select Creole Seasoning

3 tablespoons paprika
1 tablespoon black pepper
1 tablespoon cayenne pepper
1 tablespoon onion powder
1 tablespoon ground thyme leaves

3 tablespoons salt
1 tablespoon white pepper
1 tablespoon garlic powder
1 tablespoon ground oregano

Blend together. Store in airtight container. Sprinkle on meat, fish, poultry and vegetables.

Evelyn's Best Seasoning

2 tablespoons salt
2 teaspoons Fiesta seasoning
2 teaspoons oregano
1 tablespoon Nature's Seasons
1 tablespoon celery seed
1 tablespoon garden vegetable
1 tablespoon pizza seasoning
1 tablespoon Italian seasoning
1 tablespoon garlic pepper blend

2 tablespoons dry onion
2 teaspoons cilantro
1 tablespoon dill
1 tablespoon dry bell pepper
1 tablespoon salsa seasoning
1 tablespoon lemon pepper
1 tablespoon garlic flakes
1 tablespoon garlic and spice

Put through a blender. Sprinkle on any salad or seafood or meat.

Evelyn's Seasonal Seasoning

1 tablespoon of the following dry ingredients:

salt	onion	green bell pepper
garlic	cilantro	dill
sugar	parsley	celery seed
red bell pepper	tomato	chives

1 teaspoon of the following dry ingredients:

| oregano | lemon pepper | marjoram |
| basil | fennel | |

½ teaspoon of the following dry ingredients:

| black pepper | jalapeño pepper |

Put all ingredients in blender for a few seconds. Put in airtight jar. Season meats, potato salad, other salads and seafood.

Garlic & Pepper Blend

2 teaspoons dry garlic
½ teaspoon dry red bell pepper
½ teaspoon dry green bell pepper
½ teaspoon dry yellow bell pepper

½ teaspoon black pepper
2 teaspoons dry onion
1 teaspoon brown sugar

Blend together. Put in airtight container, place in dry place. Use in casseroles, meats, salads and etc.

Evelyn's Nature's Seasoning

1 tablespoon x 1½ teaspoons black pepper
2 tablespoons salt

1 tablespoon of each of the following:

sugar	royal peppercorns
garlic salt	garlic and spice
dry onion	dry garlic
dry parsley	celery seed
garlic peppercorn blend	

Blend till fine, in blender. Use on seafood, meats, vegetables and soups. Store in airtight container.

Evelyn's Dry Marinade & Seasoning

2 teaspoons salt

1 teaspoon of each of the following:

garlic peppercorn blend	royal peppercorn blend
cracked black pepper	garlic and spice
Italian salad	pepper ranch
grill seasoning	dry mustard
garlic and herb	basil
Nature's Seasons	

Put in blender. Put in plastic bag and marinate overnight. Excellent on any food, vegetables or meats etc.

Picnic Dry Seasoning 50's (Brisket Rub)
Bar-B-Que

2 cups salt	½ cup cracked peppercorns
1 tablespoon chili powder	1 tablespoon cinnamon
1 teaspoon marjoram	Dash nutmeg and cumin

Combine all ingredients, mix well, spread the seasoning over brisket. Store any remaining seasoning in refrigerator.

Spice Blends

The spice blends may be used as a meat rub for beef, pork, chicken, or as a dip mix.

For a dip mix use 8 oz. of sour cream, 2 tablespoons mayonnaise, 1 tablespoon spice blend of your choice.

Jalapeño Blend
6 tablespoons onion powder
4 teaspoons oregano
4 teaspoons sugar
2 teaspoons jalapeño powder

3 tablespoons salt
4 teaspoons dry mustard
2 teaspoons cumin
2 teaspoons garlic powder

Makes 1 cup blend

Thyme Blend
6 tablespoons onion powder
4 teaspoons jalapeño powder
4 teaspoons cumin
2 teaspoons coriander

3 tablespoons salt
4 teaspoons sugar
4 teaspoons thyme

Makes 1 cup blend

Oregano Blend
6 tablespoons onion powder
4 teaspoons jalapeño
2 teaspoons oregano

3 tablespoons salt
4 teaspoons sugar
2 teaspoons coriander

Makes ¾ cup blend

Cumin Blend
6 tablespoons onion powder
3 tablespoons curry powder
1 teaspoon thyme

3 tablespoons salt
3 tablespoons cumin
2 teaspoons pepper

Makes 1 cup blend

Texas Pie Crust (Large)

Enough for 13 x 9 x 2-inch baking dish plus strips on top.

2 tablespoons sugar
4 cups flour
1¾ cups solid shortening
½ cup water

1 teaspoon salt
1 teaspoon baking powder
2 eggs
2 teaspoons vinegar

Mix the above together. On floured surface roll out ¾ of the dough in an 18 x 14-inch rectangle. Put in baking dish. Fill with your favorite filling. Roll remaining dough for top strips.

Garden Fresh Cabbage Slaw

3 cups thin sliced cabbage
¼ of medium green bell pepper
¼ of medium red bell pepper
2 teaspoons vinegar
1 teaspoon walnut oil
Dash of salt and pepper

1 stalk celery diced
2 tablespoons chopped onion
½ thin sliced apple
3 tablespoons mayonnaise
2 tablespoons sugar
½ teaspoon celery seed

Mix all together.

Substitutions

Ingredient called for	Substitution
1 cup self-rising flour	1 cup all-purpose flour plus 1 teaspoon baking powder and ½ teaspoon salt
1 cup cake flour	1 cup sifted all-purpose flour minus 2 tablespoons
1 cup all-purpose flour	1 cup cake flour plus 2 tablespoons
1 teaspoon baking powder	½ teaspoon cream of tartar plus ¼ teaspoon soda
1 tablespoon tapioca	1½ tablespoons all-purpose flour
8 oz. sour cream	1 tablespoon lemon juice plus evaporated milk to equal 1 cup
1 cup yogurt	1 cup buttermilk or sour milk
1 cup sour milk or buttermilk	1 tablespoon vinegar plus milk to equal 1 cup
1 cup fresh milk	½ cup evaporated milk plus ½ cup water
1 (1-oz.) square chocolate	3 tablespoons cocoa plus 1 tablespoon butter
1 tablespoon fresh herbs	1 teaspoon dried herbs or ¼ teaspoon powdered herbs
1 teaspoon dry mustard	1 tablespoon prepared mustard

Note: 1 egg equals 2 egg whites, and 2 eggs equals ½ cup egg substitute.

Quick cooking oats, browned in a small amount of butter, makes a substitute for chopped nuts in a cookie recipe.

For some icing recipes you may substitute condensed milk for whipping cream.

Thought:
If you are not happy with what you have now, how do you know you would be happier with more?

Thought:
If Jesus called you, and said he would be at your house in 3 minutes, could you just sit down and wait for him? Or would you have to rush around and clean the house first?

Index